Wonder zone

Discovering God's wonderful world

A Bible-based holiday club from **Scripture Union** and **The Faraday Institute** for 5- to 11-year-olds

© Scripture Union 2019

First published 2019

ISBN 978 1 78506 743 3

Scripture Union
Trinity House, Opal Court, Opal Drive,
Fox Milne, Milton Keynes MK15 0DF
Email: info@scriptureunion.org.uk
Website: www.scriptureunion.org.uk

All rights reserved. No part of this publication may be reproduced, stored in a retrieval system, or transmitted in any form or by any means, electronic, mechanical, photocopying, recording or otherwise, without the prior permission of Scripture Union.

The right of Alex Taylor to be identified as the author of this work has been asserted by him in accordance with the Copyright, Designs and Patents Act.

Scripture quotations are from the Contemporary English Version published by HarperCollins*Publishers* © 1991, 1992, 1995 American Bible Society or from the *Good News Bible*, published by The Bible Societies/HarperCollins*Publishers* Ltd, UK, © American Bible Society, 1966, 1971, 1976, 1992.

British Library Cataloguing-in-Publication Data

A catalogue record of this book is available from the British Library.

Printed in India by Nutech Print - Services

Cover and internal design: kwgraphicdesign

Scripture Union is an international Christian charity working with churches in more than 130 countries.

Find out more about our work and how you can get involved at:

- www.scriptureunion.org.uk
  (England and Wales)
- www.suscotland.org.uk (Scotland)
- www.suni.co.uk (Northern Ireland)
- www.scriptureunion.org (USA)
- www.su.org.au (Australia)

Wonder Zone has been produced in collaboration with The Faraday Institute for Science and Religion. The Faraday Institute is an interdisciplinary research and communication enterprise linked to the University of Cambridge. Their Youth and Schools Team are committed to providing high-quality events and resources that encourage young people of all backgrounds to explore the interactions of science and religious faith in exciting and engaging ways. They think it's really important that all young people are able to search for answers to any and all of their questions, at any age.

- www.faraday-institute.org

This project and publication were made possible through the support of a grant from the John Templeton Foundation. The opinions expressed in this publication are those of the authors and do not necessarily reflect the views of the John Templeton Foundation.

Contents

Welcome	**4**
Pre-prep	**7**
1 Aims and Bible programme	**8**
• The aims of **Wonder Zone**	8
• The **Wonder Zone** Bible programme	9
• A shorter holiday club programme	10
2 Themes and settings	**11**
• People of **Wonder Zone**	11
• Your venue	11
3 Team roles and tasks	**13**
• Team roles	13
• Important things to remember	16
4 Planning your club	**17**
• Before and after	17
• Experiments	17
• Programme elements	18
• Publicity and admin	20
• Legal requirements and safeguarding	20
• Children with additional needs	20

The Experiments (Sessions)	**21**
Experiment 1	**22**
The fun of discovery	
Experiment 2	**29**
The wonders of the universe	
Experiment 3	**36**
The colours of the rainbow	
Experiment 4	**43**
The creatures of the world	
Experiment 5	**50**
The possibilities of robots	
Lab equipment	**57**
1 Bible story scripts	58
2 Hands on activities	63
3 Art and construction	69
4 Games activities	73
5 Drama scripts: *Discovery Team*	77
6 Other resources	88

Wonder Zone welcome

Welcome to Wonder Zone! Join your Lab and explore some great scientific discoveries. Find out who God is and how exploring science and following him can go hand in hand.

The Researchers and Lab Technicians are ready to help Scientists (the children) as they explore. Through their explorations, they'll discover the wonders of the world (and beyond!) and how the God behind all of it wants to get to know them too.

Whether beginner or boffin, you'll find your home at **Wonder Zone**!

Wonder Zone is a five-day children's holiday club, with lots of suggestions for how to expand the club to include parents, carers and families.

Go to:

For details of the aims, go to page 8.

For details of theme, setting and roles of **Wonder Zone**, go to pages 11 to 15.

For outlines for each day's session, go to pages 9 and 10.

For a resource bank of activity ideas, go to pages 63 to 76.

THE EXPERIMENTS (SESSIONS)

Experiment 1
The fun of discovery
1 Kings 3:5–15

Experiment 2
The wonders of the universe
Psalm 8

Experiment 3
The colours of the rainbow
John 9:1–34; 8:12

Experiment 4
The creatures of the world
Psalms 104; 139

Experiment 5
The possibilities of robots
Luke 15:11–32

Who is it for?

Every effort has been made to ensure this programme is suitable for children with little or no church background. It is a tool for churches whose desire is to reach out to children and families from outside their church community.

It should work equally well for churches wishing to use it as a discipleship resource for children already part of the church family.

Hints and tips are given with each session for children who are new to a faith-based club, who are used to church, who have additional needs and who have backgrounds from other faiths.

Resources to help you

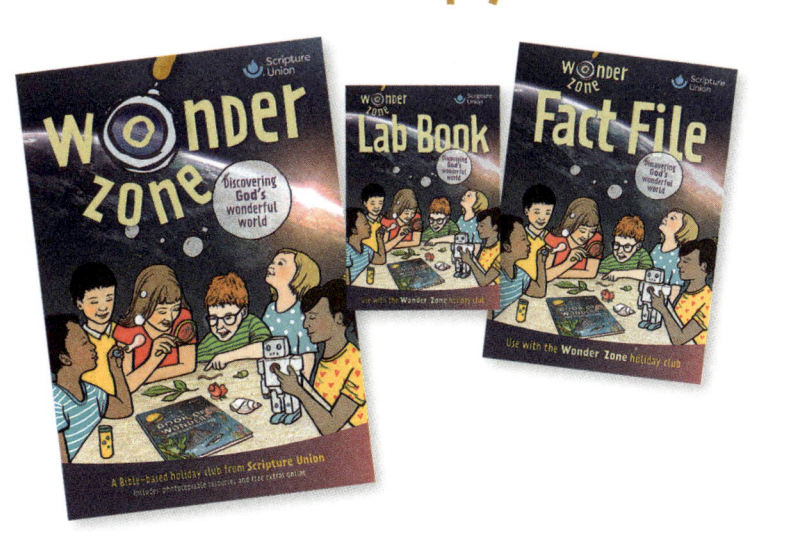

Resource book

Packed with creative ideas on how to explore and discover some of the wonders of the universe and the wonders of God. There are also ideas for experiments, construction (craft), games, drama, creative prayer and worship. **Wonder Zone** has a mixture of upfront presentation and small-group activities, allowing children and leaders to build meaningful relationships with each other and with God.

Each session or Experiment of **Wonder Zone** is designed to work as an individual event, as well as forming part of a five-session club.

Lab Book

For older children

This 48-page booklet contains all the key Bible text taken from the Contemporary English Version, along with small-group material, puzzles and extra information. It is ideal for use with 8 to 11s.

Fact File

For younger children

This 32-page booklet contains retold Bible stories, with key Bible verses taken from the Contemporary English Version, along with small-group material, puzzles and extra information, for younger children.

There are hints and tips for using both these resources as part of the small-group time in each Experiment. Both the *Lab Book* and *Fact File* help maintain contact with children's homes and act as a reminder, in the weeks after the club, of what the children experienced at **Wonder Zone**. You can buy both books as multiple copies – see the inside front cover for details.

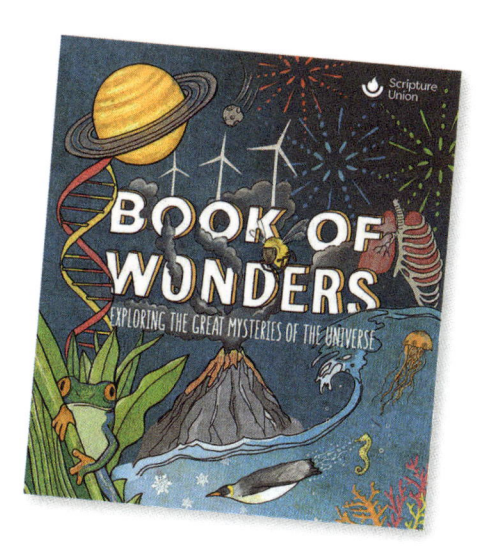

Book of Wonders

Filled with amazing details of the wonderful world God has created, information and quotes from scientists about how they meet God in their specialist field. This large-format hard-backed book, also produced in partnership with The Faraday Institute, will allow children at the club to explore for themselves the science and faith they are learning about.

Book of Wonders: Activity Book

An activity book about science and faith – an ideal gift for the children to take home at the end of **Wonder Zone**.

For more details on the *Book of Wonders* and the *Book of Wonders: Activity Book* see the inside front cover.

WELCOME

Wonder Zone multimedia downloads

To supplement your club a wealth of multimedia downloadable resources is available from the **Wonder Zone** multimedia downloads area.

www.scriptureunion.org.uk/WonderZone

Resources include:

- video retellings of the Bible stories in each Experiment
- **Wonder Zone** theme song
- printable versions of the photocopiable resources
- drama and story scripts
- administration forms
- a parallel programme for under-5s, following the same Bible passages and themes as the main programme
- a parallel programme for 11 to 14s, following the same Bible passages and themes as the main programme
- a training course for young leaders aged 14 to 18
- training sessions for your team
- follow-up ideas
- logos, posters…
- … and more!

Wonder Zone theme song

'It's a Wonderful, Wonderful World' is the **Wonder Zone** holiday club theme song.

For theme song lyrics and sheet music, go to page 93. For these plus an MP3 of the song go to the **Wonder Zone** multimedia downloads area.

Publicity materials and merchandise

See the inside back cover for details of the publicity materials produced by Christian Publicity and Outreach. (Please note, CPO resources are not available through Scripture Union.)

You don't need to be a boffin

You might not have a degree in chemical engineering or have done research with lemurs in Madagascar, but don't worry! You can still lead or volunteer in **Wonder Zone**. Part of the joy of scientific discovery is finding out new things together. However, there is a great place to go to if you are asked questions that you can't quite answer – The Faraday Institute have created a website that will help you to explore scientific themes and topics in a child-friendly way.

Faraday Kids
Science and Religion

Go to www.faradaykids.com for the chance to explore more about science, faith and what God has made. You'll find activities, videos and age-specific discussion of all sorts of interesting questions. You can also find out more about The Faraday Institute's other books, apps and videos, and share your experience of using these resources.

Faraday Educators
Science and Religion
Resources for Kids & Teens

And check out www.faradayeducators.com for more information about other resources and events.

PRE-PREP

PRE-PREP

PRE-PREP 1 — Aims and Bible programme

Wonder Zone explores lots of Bible stories that will inspire children towards scientific discoveries as well as encountering a creative God who wants to be their friend.

Through the Bible stories explored in **Wonder Zone**, the children meet Solomon and his desire to be wise. They will explore three psalms and see what those tell us about God. They'll see Jesus bring sight to a blind man and 'light for the world'. And they'll hear the story of the lost son, the choices he made that took him on his own way and the choices he made to come back to his father once more.

These Bible passages will help you make links between the kinds of thinking that inspire both science and faith, and reveal to children how science and faith can go hand in hand to help us understand the world we live in. They'll discover the different aims of science and faith and what they set out to do. And they'll meet real-life scientists and the stories of their faith.

Points to note

You might like to take some time to consider your own specific aims for your club. You can find some material in the **Wonder Zone** multimedia downloads area to help you do this.

The aims of Wonder Zone

- To help children experience the wonder and awe of scientific discovery.
- To help children experience the wonder and awe of knowing God and meeting Jesus, through exploring his creation.
- To invite children to encounter and potentially respond to God, to Jesus and to the offer of eternal life.
- To show children how a Christian community engages with relevant topics and the big questions of science and technology.
- To create lasting, positive memories of Christian community, to build relationships and help children and their families become part of a Christian community.
- To offer a safe and fun environment for all children.
- To nurture the Christian faith of all the adults who are involved in the club.

The Wonder Zone Bible programme

Each day, children encounter complementary aspects of scientific study and Bible passages. Through these, they'll see how science and faith can go hand in hand to help us explore the wonder of the world we live in and the wonder of God. This is God who, while being the Creator of everything good that exists, wants us to get to know him by believing and trusting in Jesus. Whether you do just one or all five Experiments with the children, make sure you include elements that will help children to encounter God in this way.

The Experiments (Bible teaching: day by day)

1 The fun of discovery
Solomon chooses wisdom

1 Kings 3:5–15

Aim: To have fun discovering new things about God and the world he made.

This session opens up the idea of questions of science and faith, their differences and how they can go hand in hand in helping us to understand ourselves and the world around us. The idea of 'discovery' runs through the whole session, being applied to both faith and science. Finding out something new is exciting, and the children will be invited to discover something new about the world around them, about God and about the adventure of discovery Jesus is calling them on.

2 The wonders of the universe
God creates the heavens

Psalm 8

Aim: To wonder at the scale and beauty of the universe God has created.

This session goes out into the universe. Space is something that fascinates children, and the size and scale of the universe (compared with us) is astonishing and humbling. Psalm 8 draws together the universal and the personal, and helps children to think about a God who created the universe, but is still interested in and cares for them. God is the God of the big and the small.

3 The colours of the rainbow
Jesus, the 'light for the world'

John 9:1–34; 8:12

Aim: To discover more about light, both scientifically and what Jesus meant when he called himself the 'light for the world'.

This session focuses on the effect of the sun on our world – bringing life to the world, light and colour to our lives and helping us to see the beauty around us. In this Bible passage, Jesus repeats his earlier statement that he is the 'light for the world' (see John 8:12). As the children explore light and colour, this story helps them to bridge the conceptual gap to discover something of what Jesus was talking about when he said he is the 'light for the world'.

PRE-PREP

4 The creatures of the world
God created me

Psalms 104; 139

Aim: To explore the diversity and nature of God's creation, and our place in it.

Most children love animals – both the cute ones and the ones that seem really weird – and this session will help them explore the natural world and how they fit in with it. God cares about the whole world, and that includes us. What is our reaction to that, both personally and in the way we treat the world around us? Psalm 104 will help children think about the diversity of the natural world, while Psalm 139 enables children to discover that God cares for them.

5 The possibilities of robots
The lost son

Luke 15:11–32

Aim: To discover that we have the ability to choose what we do – and to choose Jesus.

Children will have encountered robots and AI, from the simple robots you can buy in the shops to those they have discovered about at school – complex ones that can learn from experience and better follow/interpret their programming. Yet, can even the most sophisticated AI choose what they do, or must they always follow their programming? Through the familiar story of the lost son, the children will think about our ability to choose to follow Jesus or not, and what that might mean for us.

A shorter holiday club programme

If you have less time, choose whichever Experiments are most appropriate to your context. Piece together enough Experiments to fill the time you have.

How to introduce children to Jesus

We know that an encounter with Jesus can lead to a whole-life transformation, so how do you introduce Jesus to a child at your holiday club?

When you're sharing Jesus with the children at your holiday club, don't assume that they have any previous knowledge or God framework. Share your experience of knowing and following Jesus in a way that they can understand and relate to – tell personal stories of the difference Jesus has made in your life.

The goal is not primarily about behaviour change, a particular moral world view or knowledge of Bible stories, but for each child to encounter Jesus. Use the most appropriate ideas, language, format and media for the children in your holiday-club context, and remember to give lots of opportunities for them to ask questions and explore Jesus for themselves.

Science and the Bible

Almost every book of the Bible talks about God as Creator. Although the writers of the Bible passages may not have been aware of or talking about modern scientific ideas, for many hundreds of years, Bible scholars have marvelled at the richness of the many different pictures used to describe God the Creator and his relationship with his creation.

There are many different points of view about how faith and science interact and history is full of people drawn to worship God through exploring the expanse, depth and intricacies of his creation; today, all over the world, we do the same. From the youngest child to the world's top scientists, God delights in our wonder at his creation.

For a more detailed resource on science and the Bible, go to the **Wonder Zone** multimedia downloads area.

PRE-PREP 2
Themes and settings

The scientific exploration and biblical material link together naturally: each Experiment (session) covers a different area of science – chemistry, astronomy, physics, biology and zoology, robotics – and relates to the Bible content. Children will encounter God and ask questions of science and faith, and how they meet together.

There are plenty of opportunities to try out some practical science during the session; there are various upfront and small-group activities in the programme. This scientific discovery is backed up by interviews with scientists who explain their love of their field and faith. These videos are available from the **Wonder Zone** multimedia downloads area.

People of Wonder Zone

The club is led from the front by one or two Professors. The gender of these roles is not important, but try to achieve a gender balance of presenters from the front – this will show children that scientific study is not a discipline pursued only by one gender or another. Representation (seeing someone like them on stage) is a powerful thing for children.

The children become the Scientists in the club. When they arrive at **Wonder Zone**, they are assigned to a Lab, staffed by a Researcher and Lab Technicians. These are the small groups that they will be part of for the club.

The Minister of Science is the overall coordinator of the club, but might not make many appearances on stage.

Your venue

Choosing the right venue is very important. Sometimes a community hall or school is a well-equipped, neutral venue that can be non-threatening for children and parents outside the church. However, you may wish to use this opportunity to introduce children and parents to your church building. The venue needs to have enough space for the number of children and the types of activities you are planning.

For more advice on choosing a venue and adult:child ratios, go to the **Wonder Zone** multimedia downloads area and download 'Legal requirements for holiday clubs'.

Setting up the room

Your venue is a science laboratory. Dress your space with computer screens, scientific charts and scientific equipment. If you have more time and resources, create 'radioactive' areas, make elaborate scientific machines from boxes and other junk, and set up bubbling test tubes. Fill your screen with footage of volcanoes, space and other dramatic images.

Volunteers should dress in lab coats and safety goggles. You could even have people in overalls, space suits or hazard suits! Wellies or chest waders, butterfly nets and hard hats would all help to illustrate the diversity of science.

If you cannot leave your room set up from session to session, prepare pictures on display boards or large banners that can be put into place quickly at the start of each session. Make sure you allow extra time for this and have team members lined up to help.

Fill the screen

If you are using a projector to display song words, for example, use interesting images when it is not being used, so that the screen is never blank. Find the **Wonder Zone** logo and other themed artwork in the **Wonder Zone** multimedia downloads area.

Drama

You should also consider which area you will use for your drama presentation. Use whatever you can to create the **Wonder Zone** transporter – the amazing vehicle that plays a central part in the **Wonder Zone** drama. If your transporter is elaborate, you might want to leave it set up at the side of the presentation area. A raised stage is ideal to allow all the children to see the action.

Band

When deciding where to place your band, the Quarks, make sure you think about access to electricity and the safety of trailing cables and so on.

Chemical store

A draped-off area or a linking room will be useful for the drama team to emerge from. This can double as a staff room for team members.

Labs

The rest of the room can be divided into a space for each Lab. Remember, each Lab will include a Researcher (leader), a Lab Technician and six to eight Scientists.

Much will depend on whether the areas can be left from session to session. Larger spaces could mean the Labs can become more elaborate as the club progresses, with pictures and diagrams, selfies, collections of things the children have found or made and areas for sitting and working.

Scientists' staff room

Some children can find the busy atmosphere of a holiday club a bit overwhelming, and some need time and quiet to process what they have seen and heard. Create a Time Out area for children to go to when they don't want to take part in a particular activity, such as scientific experiments, construction or games. Include beanbags, pens and paper, and make sure leaders are available to chat to any children who have a question (keep in mind your church safeguarding policy).

Encourage the children to keep on discovering during this time by providing the *Book of Wonders*, open at the relevant pages, and other books and information on the day's science topic and Bible passage.

Make sure you affirm any child who wants to use the Time Out area – this is just as valid a way of participating in the holiday club as any other.

Venue maps

Once you have decided the locations within your venue, give each team member a map to remind them of what is happening where – and so they can work out where they need to be at any given time in the session. Include emergency exits, toilets and 'no entry' areas on the map, too.

PRE-PREP 3

Team roles and tasks

These pages will take you through all the roles and functions that will help your club run smoothly. Not all have to happen at the holiday club, or all the time the club is running, so individuals may take on several roles and functions.

We have noted which roles we see as essential, if you have a small team, and those that are great to have, if you are blessed with a larger team. Remember, you do not need a different person for each role – and many roles are optional: the club will still work without them. The larger and more experienced your team, the more options and activities you can offer, but don't be put off by small numbers. Work and adapt with what you've got.

Team roles

The table on pages 14 and 15 shows all the roles you may choose to use in your holiday club. More detail on team roles and tasks, should you need it, is available from the **Wonder Zone** multimedia downloads area, along with job descriptions for each role. The specific characters mentioned in the sessions are:

The Professors

The main presenters of **Wonder Zone**. Together, they guide children through the session, introducing the different elements, helping to tell the Bible story and delivering the teaching for the day.

Researchers and Lab Technicians

These are the leaders of each Lab (small group) and those helping them. The Researcher has responsibility for the Scientists (children) in the Lab.

Team roles and functions

Role	Function	Essential/Optional
Core planning team	Small group to lead organising the club	Essential
Minister of Science	Overall leader of the holiday club	Essential
The Professors	Main presenters	Essential
Researchers	Small group leaders	Essential
Lab Technicians	Junior leaders or helpers	Optional
Keycode team	Registration: books children in; keeps records	Essential
Quarks	Live worship band	Optional
Drama leader	Recruits drama team; runs daily drama	Optional
Experiments coordinator	Organises all scientific experiments at the club	Optional
Games coordinator	Organises all games activities at the club	Optional
Construction/craft organiser	Organises hands-on creative activities	Optional
Canteen head cook and team	Makes sure refreshments happen on time and safely	Essential
First-aider	As required; maintains records	Essential
Technical manager	Makes sure everything works as and when it should	Optional, depending on what you are using
Publicity and admin person or team	Publicise the club; club paperwork	Optional
Health and safety person	Ensures safety of everyone at the club	Preferable
Meeters and greeters	Available to chat to adults as they bring and collect their children	Optional
Prayer team	Prays	Essential

Upfront/Behind the scenes	Special skills	Team members
Behind the scenes		
Behind the scenes	Organisation, monitoring, leading	
Upfront	Confident, able to engage and involve children	
A bit of both	Leading small groups of children	
A bit of both	Willing to learn and join in	
Both	Attention to detail, welcoming and friendly	
Upfront	Musical, leading worship	
Both	Acting and team leading	
Either or both	Enthusiasm, attention to detail	
Either or both	Energy and enthusiasm	
Either or both	Creativity and patience	
Behind the scenes	Organisation and planning	
Behind the scenes	Current first-aid qualification	
Behind the scenes	Practical and technical	
Behind the scenes		
Behind the scenes	Risk assessments	
A bit of both	Welcoming, friendly and reassuring	
Behind the scenes		

Important things to remember

Ratios and training
Under-18s count as children, when you're working out adult:child ratios. If you have a lot of Lab Technicians helping in Labs, you will need more Researchers, rather than fewer.

All team members should be given training in dealing with children, especially in relation to physical contact and not being with children alone out of sight of others, but Researchers and Lab Technicians especially need to be aware of child protection issues and safeguarding policies.

Forward planning
If possible, encourage parents of children to complete booking forms in advance to be returned to the leader of the holiday club, school office or community group leader. This means you can allocate children to Labs in advance and you will already be aware of dietary requirements, medical issues and physical, educational or behavioural special needs. Remember to check these when planning the club activities!

On-the-day registration
In some contexts, pre-registering is not practical: ensure that on the first day there are plenty of extra volunteers available to help greet the children and their parents or carers and to provide them with the registration form to fill in. Children should not attend the event if permission has not been granted. As this can be a lengthy process, you should open the doors earlier on the first day. If the registration process is extended, engage the children in parachute games, upfront games or a short film. (For game suggestions, go to pages 73 to 76 or search online.)

Data protection
Whether booking forms are completed before the club or on the day, you must collect and store the data provided in accordance with the General Data Protection Regulation (GDPR).

Identification
- Each team member should have an appropriate, clearly labelled badge to identify them and their role.
- The children registered for **Wonder Zone** should each have their own badge, which should be taken off before they leave the club.
- Any adult or child on site not wearing an appropriate badge should be challenged.
- Each child can be given a new sticky-backed badge each day, when they register.

Think about

A group of people to source the necessary materials will be invaluable, especially in the run-up to **Wonder Zone**. They can make templates and patterns for children to draw around or cut out, help produce prototypes of each design and pass on any hints to the Researchers.

Involve local schools in amassing reusable material to use during the club (such as yogurt pots, plastic bottles or other 'junk' for modelling). This actively involves people in contributing to the club before it has begun, including the children, and alerts the school to the club's existence, bringing extra publicity.

PRE-PREP 4

Planning your club

Before and after

You might wish to theme the church services before and after your club to complement the activities and teaching from the five club sessions. Use elements of the Experiments (sessions) to give people a taster and reminder of **Wonder Zone**.

Give some consideration to how you are going to connect new children and families into the life of your church community. A church service after the club gives you a natural connection to encourage children from outside your church community and their families into church.

Services could be at the same time as your usual Sunday service, or at a different time or even on a different day.

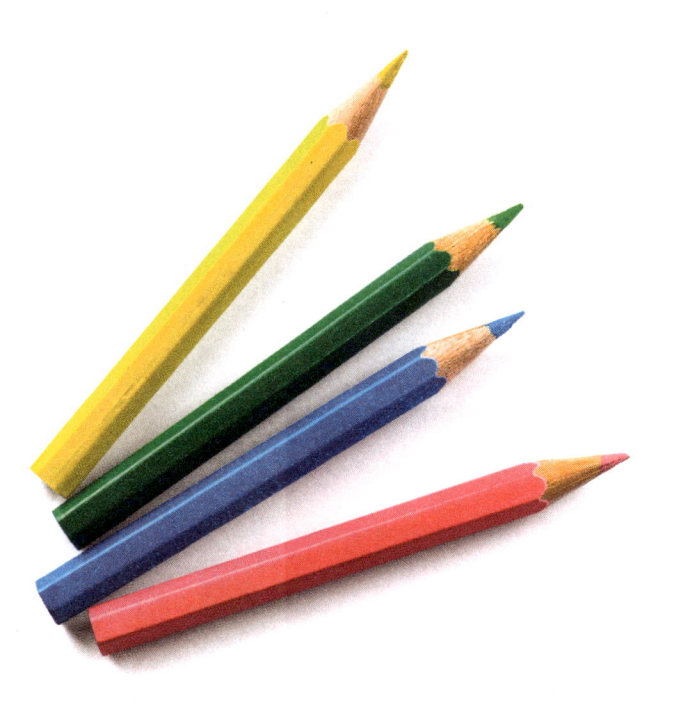

Experiments

The Experiments in **Wonder Zone** follow a regular pattern that has been popular with many groups, but you don't have to follow this pattern! Plan your programme for your club!

- Decide on the mix of all-together and small-group time that will work well with your venue, timing and numbers.
- Select which programme elements are most important for you, and put these into your programme first.
- Fit other activities around these core essentials.
- Arrange at least one training-and-preparation session for your team before the club. Go to the **Wonder Zone** multimedia downloads area for training modules and tips.
- Select the activities according to the children you are likely to have at the club: they should be the most important consideration when choosing the daily activities. Children respond differently to the same activity. (Researchers, in particular, should bear this in mind when planning activities for their Lab.)
- If you have a long club session, then you will be able to do more! The timings given are merely guidelines; different children will take different lengths of time to complete the same activity.
- Have something in your programme you can drop if things overrun.

Small-group time: Get exploring

Within each Experiment, children will spend time in small groups (Labs). Part of this time is likely to be spent in scientific exploration, construction and games: suitable activities are in Lab equipment (see pages 63 to 76). There are two popular ways to run these: chat with your team about what will work well for your club.

1. Every Lab does the same game or activity during the same session. This requires a lot of resources and may limit the type of activity you use. It is easy to theme the activity closely with the Bible and science learning.

2. Certain activities are set up every session and the Labs rotate around them. This needs fewer resources and an extra leader can run the activity, while the Researchers have more time to interact with their Lab; but your venue may not be large enough.

Programme elements

In summary

Programme elements are listed in the table on page 19: the Experiments, starting on page 21, give you activity material for each of these elements, every day of the club. Tick the ones you plan to use in your club – and remember, you can rearrange them in your own order. (We've put in a few ticks to start you off.)

For a two-hour club session, a popular timetable has a few minutes in small groups while everyone arrives; followed by a 45-minute all-together time; the children then do activities in small groups for another 45 minutes; then come back together for a 20-minute all-together finish.

To view detailed instructions for each element of the programme go to the **Wonder Zone** multimedia downloads area.

Research kit

Each Experiment contains a list of specific items needed that day. The following list of items will be needed for all Experiments:

- registration forms, badges, labels, pens, team lists
- scientist videos
- a set of risk-assessed warm-up exercises
- the Quarks band or backing tracks
- a postbox – called the Large Hadron Collider
- storytelling script, costumes
- video storytelling episode
- drinks and snacks
- copies of the *Book of Wonders*
- copies of *Lab Book*
- copies of *Fact File*
- Bibles, paper, pens, pencils, felt-tip pens or crayons
- equipment for your chosen scientific experiment(s)
- materials for your chosen construction(s)
- equipment for your chosen game(s)
- items for the Time Out area, such as beanbags, pens, paper
- quiz questions and challenges
- drama scripts, costumes and props
- *Learn and remember* verse PowerPoint

Programme elements

Title	What it is	Time	Children	Team	Tick
Doing your research	Team preparation	30 minutes		Whole team	✓
Registration	Registration		Individually	Keycode team	✓
Lab prep	Settling in; building relationships	10 minutes	Small groups	Researchers and Lab Technicians	
Let's investigate	Welcome	45 minutes	Everyone together	The Professors	✓
Big bang	Setting the scene			The Professors	
Check your equipment	Warming-up exercises			Lab Technicians	
Lab sing song	Theme song and more			Quarks	
Lab practice	Themed experiment			The Professors	✓
Large Hadron Collider	Postbox			The Professors	
Exploring the evidence	Bible storytelling			The Professors	
Observations	Theme song			The Professors	
Under the microscope	Group time	25 minutes	Small groups	Researchers and Lab Technicians	
The canteen	Refreshments			Canteen head cook and team	✓
Test your findings	Bible discovery			Researchers	✓
Time to wonder	Prayer			Researchers	✓
Get exploring	Experiments/ construction/craft/ games	20 minutes	Small groups	Researchers and Lab Technicians	
Check your results		20 minutes	Everyone together	The Professors	
A scientist's view	Video				
The appliance of science	Facts-based quiz				
Discovery Team	Drama			Drama team	
The knowledge	*Learn and remember* verse			The Professors	
Put your heads together	Praying together			The Professors	✓
Conclusions	Wrap-up of the day				
Final findings	Waiting to go	10 minutes	Small groups	Researchers and Lab Technicians	
Decon chamber	Clear up; debrief	30 minutes		Whole team	

Publicity and admin

Ensure you have plenty of children at your holiday club through effective use of publicity and promotional materials.

Plan this as carefully as other aspects of your club: it's easy to spend a lot of time and money without getting your message to those you want to hear and respond. Don't forget to advertise your club through your regular church newsletters, services and social media channels.

The following publicity materials are available from the **Wonder Zone** multimedia downloads area, or via CPO (see inside back cover):

- posters/flyers
- direct letters or invitation cards
- school assemblies
- press releases.

The following administrative forms are available from the **Wonder Zone** multimedia downloads area:

- club aims form
- evaluation form
- collection slips.

Legal requirements and safeguarding

There are various legal requirements you will need to be familiar with and conform to as you prepare for your holiday club. You will need to consider the following:

- safeguarding and child protection policies
- provision of adequate space in your venue
- meeting adult:child ratios
- registering your club
- insurance
- data protection (GDPR)
- accidents and first aid
- issues of health and safety, including risk assessments
- fire procedures and guidelines
- food hygiene.

To obtain up-to-date information on all of these requirements, go to 'Legal requirements for running a club' in the **Wonder Zone** multimedia downloads area.

Children with additional needs

It is quite possible you will have children with any combination of additional needs attending your holiday club.

There are a few things you can do in advance that will help these children to settle more quickly:

- Make sure you have as much useful information about the children as possible before the holiday club starts. Find out from parents or carers what would help their child the most.
- Invite children who struggle with change to arrive early so they can look around, meet leaders and settle in before all the other children arrive.
- It's also helpful to give a basic outline, in order, of the daily activities to the parents or carers of these children, and ask if they can help you produce a visual timetable for their child.
- Make sure you have alternative formats of words and visuals you show on screens for children who won't be able to see or read them. Find out the best format for the children who may need them.
- Make sure the way your rooms are set out allows easy wheelchair access without having to move lots of chairs or tables out of the way.
- Have leaders available who can buddy children who need one-to-one care.
- Try to allocate a quiet room for children who need 'space' from time to time.

THE EXPERIMENTS

THE EXPERIMENTS

EXPERIMENT 1

The fun of discovery

Research notes

Bible passage
1 Kings 3:5–15

Aim
To have fun discovering new things about God and the world he made.

Experiment summary
This session opens up the idea of science and faith, their differences and how they can go hand in hand in helping us to understand ourselves and the world around us. The idea of 'discovery' runs through the whole session, being applied to both faith and science. Finding out something new is exciting, and the children will be invited to discover something new about the world around them, about God and about the adventure of discovery Jesus is calling them on.

Background

Children with no church background
Many children with no experience of faith will have picked up the idea that science and faith may be in conflict, that there can be no interaction between the two or that they don't mix. However, this session sets a positive and affirming tone for both science and faith. It opens up the joy of discovery in both fields.

Church children
Church children may have been told that faith and science don't mix, by people from both outside and within the church. Help them to see that God wants us to be wise and discover amazing things about his world, as well as about our relationship with him. Neither faith nor science are static, 'take it or leave it' things.

Children of other faiths
Just as there are many different points of view about faith and science in Christianity, so there are differences in other religions too. Children will have a variety of ideas themselves, so listen carefully to what they say, while starting off the club in a positive, inclusive manner.

Children with additional needs
Children on the autistic spectrum may have a deep interest in science, whether it's engineering, dinosaurs, outer space or any number of other subjects. Share their delight in such knowledge and interest! Help them to see how ideas of faith can sit alongside their interests and be complementary to them. Explore the idea that through the science they love, they are getting to learn more about how God works.

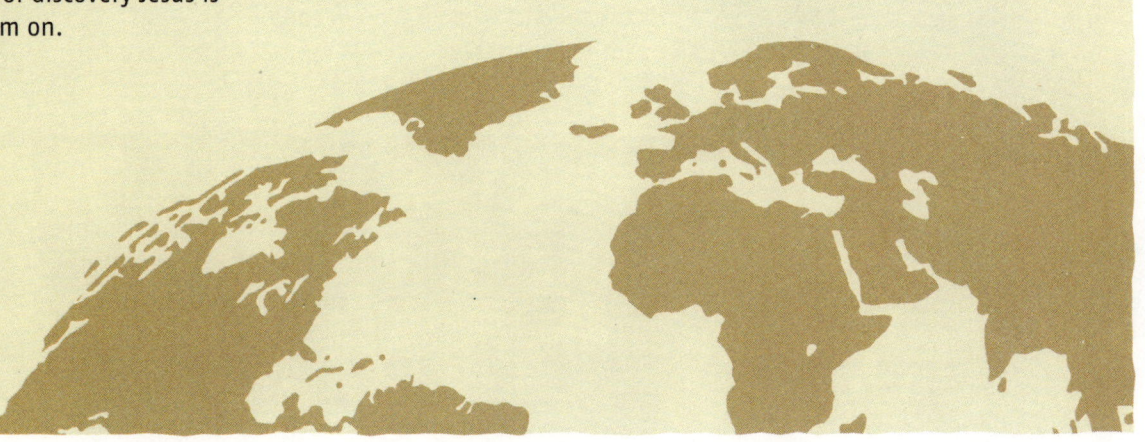

1 • THE FUN OF DISCOVERY

Doing your research

As you gather together before the session, ask the team: 'If you could have anything you like, what would it be?'

Chat about the question in small groups and then come back together for some feedback. Read 1 Kings 3 together and then go back into small groups to think about these questions:

- How would you have responded to God's question?
- What value do you give to wisdom in your own lives, your church and your community?
- How do you exercise and pursue wisdom in your walk with Christ?
- How do you think wisdom and knowledge relate?
- How and why would you encourage children to seek wisdom?

Go on to get some feedback from the group.

At the start of this session, and of **Wonder Zone** as a whole, it's important to reflect on our own walk with Jesus. If we're inviting children on his adventure of discovery, we need to evaluate our own relationship with him. Ask the small groups these questions:

- How curious are you about Jesus?
- When did you last discover something new about God? Share it with the group now.
- What are you expecting to discover yourself at **Wonder Zone**?

Encourage the Researchers and Lab Technicians to get together in their Labs and pray for the Scientists (children) who are going to be part of their group. If children are already registered, the leaders can pray for them by name. If not, they can simply thank God for the children who will be joining them and pray that they discover something about him today.

Come back together and sing some of the songs that you'll be singing as part of the club.

Then, send the team off to do the practical preparation needed for today's session.

Points to note

Sometimes views on certain areas of scientific study and research can be very emotive.

Recognise that we all might have different views on certain areas of research (eg GM foods and the wider ethical questions around genetics; animal testing).

Reflect together about how you as a team can exercise grace and love in discussions around these subjects.

What-you-need

- **Research kit**: items from the list on page 18
- **Lab prep**: a copy of the periodic table, materials for making badges
- **Lab practice**: a 2-litre bottle of room-temperature diet cola, a packet of chewy mints (such as Mentos), a test tube or roll of paper, a small piece of card, lots of clean-up equipment
- **Time to wonder**: sticky notes, large sheets of paper
- **Hands on**: items for the film canister rocket experiment (page 63)
- **Construction**: items for making splash paintings (page 70)
- **Games**: items for playing exploding canisters or fact finding (page 73)

The core experiment

Lab prep

10 minutes in small groups

Welcome all the Scientists to your group. Show the children a copy of the periodic table (you can download one from the internet or use a tablet). Explain that this is a chart of all the elements – the building blocks of the universe. Everything is made of these elements, including us! Ask the Scientists if they can spot their initials in the table. Try to make up the initials of the group. If that's not possible (and it won't be if you have children whose names start with J or Q), then ask the Scientists to choose symbols that reflect their interests or even invent their own chemical symbol.

For example, someone called Karim Ahmed could take the symbols for krypton and americium to create KrAm. Someone who loves Beyoncé might choose RnB (radon and boron). Or someone called Jenny Quinn might create her own symbols to make JnQn. Help the Scientists design badges for themselves that look like one of the elements in the table. They could include their own symbol, name and age, as well as anything else they would like to.

If you have time, come up with a name and chemical symbol for your Lab as well as for the Scientists.

Have the *Book of Wonders* available, open at pages 8 to 15, and encourage the Scientists to begin to explore today's topic for themselves.

Let's investigate!

45 minutes all together

Once all the Scientists and the team are settled, the Professors should introduce themselves and welcome everyone to **Wonder Zone**. Make sure everyone knows what to do in a fire and where the toilets are. Include any guidelines you want the Scientists to follow while they are part of **Wonder Zone**. Invite some Scientists up to the stage to show the badges they made in Lab prep. How have they described themselves with their symbols?

Big bang

At the start of the session the Professors should chat about what they like about various scientific fields – the explosiveness of some chemistry, the far-out world of astronomy or the practical elements of conservation and ecology that they can get involved in every day. Introduce the theme for today – the fun of discovery.

Ask the Scientists what amazing things they have discovered in a science class or when they were doing science-y stuff at home.

Show the film of the session's scientist talking about what they love about their field of study and the excitement they have when they discover something new.

Check your equipment

Invite a couple of Lab Technicians to the front to lead the club in a physical warm-up. The warm-up should be made up of simple actions that the Scientists can do safely. They should also take into consideration those who might have restricted movement.

Lab sing song

Introduce the band, the Quarks (if you're using them). Say that quarks are tiny sub-atomic elementary particles. They come in six flavours: top, bottom, up, down, strange and charm. Have fun deciding who in the group is the up quark, the top quark and even the strange quark!

Explain that each time the children come to **Wonder Zone**, you're going to sing some songs together. Sing the **Wonder Zone** theme song, together with any actions that you have come up with. Sing it a couple of times so the Scientists begin to get the hang of it.

Lab practice

Introduce Lab practice, a time when you can all get exploring! This session is all about the fun of discovery, so this experiment is fun, giving the children the chance to predict what might happen and then discover if they were right. Moreover, it can be quite spectacular, so should be a memorable opening to your club.

To do this experiment you need a 2-litre bottle of room-temperature diet cola, a packet of chewy mints (such as Mentos), a test tube or roll of paper, a small piece of card and lots of clean-up equipment. (You can also get a gadget to help with this – search 'geyser tube' online.) This can be a very messy experiment, so it's best to do this outside (or at least cover your indoor venue up well!).

Set your bottle of diet cola on the ground (you might want to tape it to the floor so that it doesn't tip over) and take the top off. Position all the Scientists about 5 metres away. Place three chewy mints into the test tube or roll of paper.

Explain that you're going to tip the mints into the cola. Ask the Scientists if they can guess what might happen next, and get some feedback. Some may already know the experiment or at least guess that it'll be messy!

Cover the end of the tube/roll of paper with the card, tip it over and place the tube, card end down, directly over the open top of the bottle. Pull the card away, letting the mints drop into the diet cola. The fizzy pop should quickly foam up and shoot out of the bottle creating a fountain that goes high in the air. You will need to move quickly to avoid being covered in cola!

Once you have cleaned up the mess (or gone inside), explain the scientific background to the experiment. It works because of something called nucleation. The surface of the mint is covered with lots of tiny bumps and these are ideal places for gas bubbles to form. The fact that there are so many nucleation sites and that the mints sink to the bottom means a lot of gas is created in a small area. This causes a massive build-up of pressure which results in the cola fountain!

If you can't do this live, do the experiment before the session and film it, or show an online video (search for 'coke geyser'). It might be useful to watch one of the online videos and then practise beforehand, so that you're ready for what will happen when you do it in front of the children.

You could extend this experiment by using different-sized bottles and asking the children to predict what they think will happen with each one. Warn the children not to do this at home, unless they work with their parents or carers!

Large Hadron Collider

Explain that you'd like the Scientists to take part in **Wonder Zone** by feeding their comments, questions, pictures and jokes into the Large Hadron Collider. Encourage everyone to put something in the Collider today! (If you have time, show some photos of the Collider in Switzerland – go to the **Wonder Zone** multimedia downloads section for some images.)

Exploring the evidence

The Professors introduce the evidence from the Bible about the pursuit of wisdom and knowledge, and the fun of discovering new things about the world around us, and about God too!

Each day three options are suggested for telling the Bible story. You can use the same approach each time, mix and match how you tell the story or combine the storytelling script (or your own retelling) with the film. This repetition will help the children start to think around the story and come to some conclusions.

1. The Professors retell the story using the script on pages 58 and 59. Today, the interview is with King Solomon; make sure you have rehearsed it before the session.

2. The Professors tell the story from 1 Kings 3:5–15, using their own words and personal storytelling style.

3. The Professors introduce today's video storytelling episode, available to download from the **Wonder Zone** multimedia downloads area. (If you are using option 1 or 2 together with the video, then tell the story first so that the children already have the outline of events before they watch the episode.)

Observations

After the story, the Professors should wonder about the story, focusing on these points:

- When we do experiments, we learn things about the world around us, both big and small. Scientists have a thirst for knowledge!
- Solomon could choose anything in the world and he chose to be wise. God rewarded him with lots of other things too.
- All throughout the Bible, the writers say how amazing it is to be wise and talk about the fun of discovering new things about God and the world he made.
- You don't start following God and know everything about him immediately. Being a friend of God means a life of exciting exploration and discovery. And it's the same with science: when we learn about science, it can be a lifetime of discovery!

The Professors should share their favourite scientific and faith discoveries, then send all the Scientists back to their Labs to put everything under the microscope!

Under the microscope

25 minutes in small groups

The canteen

The Researchers and Lab Technicians should make sure all the Scientists have made it back to the correct Labs. As this is the first session, spend a moment welcoming the children to the Lab, particularly if they missed Lab prep. Hand round the refreshments and chat about what the children have discovered so far.

Test your findings: Bible exploration

With older children (8 to 11s)
Give out copies of *Lab Book* and read the different facts on page 6. Give the Scientists a minute or so to write down any other facts they know. Share some of those facts together and be amazed by the discoveries you make.

Give out some felt-tip pens and read the story from page 8. As they follow the passage, encourage the Scientists to underline bits of the story that they like and draw a circle around anything that surprises them. (If you have reluctant readers in your group, pair those children with a Lab Technician.) Once you have finished, go through what the Scientists have underlined and circled.

Ask the group what they would have asked for if God had given them the choice of anything they wanted. What do they think of Solomon's choice? Remind the children that when Solomon was making his choice, he didn't know God was going to give him lots of extra things.

Share with the Lab about how you love to discover new things about God. It doesn't matter how long you have been following him, there's always something new to discover.

Chat about the different things they might want to find out about science and God at **Wonder Zone**. Point out that you're all probably hoping to find out different things about science and God. Draw out that faith and science seek to explore different aspects of the same thing: life and the world around us. While these aspects are different, they complement each other. If it's helpful, use the example of a boiling kettle: the answer to the question 'why is the kettle boiling?' can involve the mechanism or scientific aspects, eg how the kettle boils involves electricity, a heating element and the energy transferred to the water. But, if we want to come to a fuller

1 ● THE FUN OF DISCOVERY

understanding of the question, it can also be important to think about meaning and purpose-based answers, eg 'Because I want a cup of tea!'

With younger children (5 to 8s)
Do the spot the difference activity on page 5 of *Fact File* and chat with the children about what kinds of science they have done. What have they discovered? Have some simple science facts to hand to share if the children are interested (you could use the ones on page 6 of *Lab Book*).

Read the Bible story on page 6 (or read 1 Kings 3:5–8 from a Bible – the Contemporary English Version is used in *Fact File*). Answer the three questions; encourage a bit of discussion about what the children think. Read the rest of the story from page 7 (or read 1 Kings 3:9–15 from a Bible) and compare the Scientists' thoughts with what happened. Give some time for the children to write or draw in the space their own ideas about wisdom. If the children are struggling, ask them to think about what being wise might mean in their own lives.

Finally, review what you have discovered so far today and ask the Scientists what they would like to discover next. Chat about the children's ideas as they write or draw them in the space on page 8. Compare your ideas! Use these ideas as a prompt for *Time to Wonder*.

Time to wonder
Give each Scientist a sticky note and ask them to write or draw something that they have discovered today, or something they'd like to find out about while they come to **Wonder Zone**. Together, stick the sticky notes on to a large sheet of paper in a fountain shape (like the diet cola fountain the children saw in Lab practice). If any children want to share what they have written or drawn, invite them to do so. Then finish with a prayer thanking God for new things discovered and asking him to help you discover more.

Get exploring!
20 minutes in different activities

Hands on
Choose one or more of the experiments on pages 63 to 68 for the Scientists to do. 'Film canister rockets' is the most suitable, but select whichever you have the resources and space for. Enjoy exploring what happens!

Construction
Show the Scientists your art and craft materials and encourage them to create whatever they like. Alternatively, choose one of the construction ideas from pages 70 to 72; 'Splash paintings' is the most suitable, but select whichever you have the resources and space for.

Games
Choose one or more of the games from pages 73 to 76 to play; 'Exploding canisters' and 'Fact finding' are the most suitable, but select whichever you have the resources and space for.

Scientists' staff room
Ask a few Researchers and Lab Technicians to be in your Time Out area, so that any Scientists who would like to hang out and chat have the chance to do so.

Encourage the children to keep on discovering during this time by providing the *Book of Wonders*, open at pages 8 to 15, and copies of the *Book of Wonders: Activity Book*.

Check your results
20 minutes all together

Call all the Scientists back together and sing the **Wonder Zone** song. Read out any jokes or questions that Scientists have put into the Large Hadron Collider.

27

A scientist's view

Show the film of a scientist describing the excitement of discovering Jesus and what it's like to find out new things about him every day. Alternatively, ask a Researcher or Lab Technician (or someone from your congregation who is a scientist but isn't part of the club) to come to the front and talk about when they first discovered Jesus. (Go through what they are going to say before the session, so that they are confident and happy, and you're sure that it will be suitable for the children in your club.)

The appliance of science

Devise a quiz with questions about what has happened at **Wonder Zone** today – include events at the club as well as questions about the Bible story and experiments, and some physical challenges too. Play in Labs or split the Scientists into two, playing one side of your space against the other. Make it light-hearted and not too competitive!

Drama: Discovery Team

Introduce the drama. Today the Discovery team are sent by the Prof to investigate a volcano in Iceland, but they don't check the data before they go and get themselves in danger!

The knowledge

On a PowerPoint slide, display the words of the *Learn and remember* verse:

'I praise you because of the wonderful way you created me. Everything you do is marvellous! Of this I have no doubt.'
Psalm 139:14 (CEV)

Say the verse through a few times together and then challenge the Scientists to see if they can learn it before the next time **Wonder Zone** happens!

Put your heads together

Play some lively music and ask the Scientists to jump around like some of the explosions they have seen today. Then, get everyone to jump up at once and shout: 'Thank you, God!' Invite some Scientists, Researchers and Lab Technicians to come to the front to say thank you to God for the things they have discovered today. This could be something scientific they have discovered or something about God – try to get a mixture, so that you make it normal to thank God for the wonderful stuff we discover with science. After each contribution, ask everyone to shout, 'Thank you, God!'

Conclusions

Briefly recap what you have discovered in today's session Thank everyone for their super scientific skills and then send the children back to their Labs to be collected by their parents or carers.

Final findings

10 minutes in small groups

Chat with the Scientists about what you explored earlier in your Lab. As the Scientists wait to be collected, they can complete any unfinished pages from their *Lab Books* or *Fact Files*. Alternatively, you could work on any unfinished construction projects or revisit your experiments. Make sure everyone knows the next time you'll be meeting together. Say goodbye to each Scientist by name as they leave.

Decon chamber

It may be that some of the team have their own children at **Wonder Zone** and are unable to stay for long when the programme ends. Try to call everyone together to check any problems, briefly reminding them of the next session's activities and pray for the Holy Spirit to be at work in the children.

If you have time and the facilities, the team could share lunch together to round off the day.

EXPERIMENT 2

The wonders of the universe

Research notes

Bible passage
Psalm 8

Aim
To wonder at the scale and beauty of the universe God has created.

Experiment summary
This session goes out into the universe. Space is something that fascinates most children, and the size and scale of the universe (compared with us) is astonishing and humbling. Psalm 8 draws together the universal and the personal, and helps children to think about a God who created the universe, but is still interested in and cares for them. God is the God of the big and the small.

Background

Children with no church background
Children from outside a church community may never have considered a divine force in the creation of the universe. That this divine force (God!) is interested in them and cares about them might be an even bigger revelation. Help children explore this idea, and give them space to make a response to God.

Church children
For church children, the idea that the Big Bang and God's creativity aren't mutually exclusive might be a surprise to them. Help them consider that they can enjoy both the wonder of God's creation and the joy of scientific discovery about space and the universe. Discoveries in astronomy or astrophysics can cause us to praise God, just like the writer of psalms in the Bible praised God.

Children of other faiths
Most faiths have creation stories as part of their scripture or tradition. Children of other faiths will be comfortable with the idea of a supernatural hand (or more than one) behind the creation of the universe. However, they may have been taught different things about the 'who' and 'how' of this idea. They also may not have considered that the creator wants to have a personal relationship with them. Be sensitive to this, listening to their ideas and always being ready to listen to their questions about the different ideas being presented through **Wonder Zone**.

Children with additional needs
Make sure you have lots of different, sensory ways to explore the universe. For example, if you're watching films about the solar system, make sure children with visual impairment can still engage. If you're doing the solar system experiment, consider carefully how a child who struggles with movement might get involved.

THE EXPERIMENTS

What-you-need

- **Research kit**: items from the list on page 18

- **Lab prep**: a map of the stars

- **Lab practice**: a video of the creation of the universe (link available in the **Wonder Zone** downloads area), a giant tub of water, a paddle or large stick, course ground pepper

- **Exploring the evidence**: printed copies of Psalm 8, Psalm 8 PowerPoint, items for junk modelling

- **Test your findings**: pictures of the planets

- **Time to wonder**: torches or glow sticks

- **Hands on**: items for the DIY solar system experiment (page 64)

- **Construction**: items for making space and stars (page 71)

- **Games**: items for playing solar system target bowls or black hole (page 74)

- **The knowledge**: balloons

- **Put your heads together**: balloons

Doing your research

Split the team up into smaller groups and ask them to think about the different aspects of creation that fill them with awe and wonder. Encourage them to tell the others in their group about a place that they have visited that caused them to praise God for his creativity, power and glory. Challenge each small group to put together all the suggestions into a psalm-like poem.

Bring the groups back together and ask for some volunteers to read out their poem of praise to the creator God. Read Psalm 8 to the group and discuss these questions back in small groups:

- What was it about the places you put in your poem that filled you with awe?
- What does this psalm say about our place in creation?
- What does that say about God's view of us?
- What's your reaction to this?

Ask for some feedback about these questions. Then have a time of quiet and ask the team to think about whether there are times in their lives when God has especially shown his care for them (as in verse 4). What did God do and how did he do it? Think more specifically about what God did when he sent Jesus. Thinking about this will help the Researchers and Lab Technicians to consider how they might tell their own story of following Jesus to the Scientists in their group.

Finally, ask the team to get together in their Labs and pray for the children in their group.

Then, send the team off to do the practical preparation needed for today's session.

The core experiment

Lab prep
10 minutes in small groups

Welcome all the Scientists to your group. Make a special welcome to any children who are new to the club today. Show the children a map of the stars (you could look at some of the images on www.hubblesite.org/images/gallery). Spend some time looking at it and trying to guess how many stars they can see on the map. Say that when we look at the night sky there are between 5,000 and 10,000 stars visible without a telescope. If the children know any names of stars, see if you can find them on the map.

Ask the children if they know any names of constellations (stick to astronomy; don't let the conversation divert into astrology!). Encourage the Scientists to come up with a constellation to represent their Lab. Draw one out together and display it in your Lab space.

Have the *Book of Wonders* available, open at pages 16 to 25, and encourage the Scientists to begin to explore today's topic for themselves.

Let's investigate!
45 minutes all together

Once all the Scientists and the team are settled, the Professors should introduce themselves and welcome everyone to **Wonder Zone**. Remind everyone what to do in a fire and where the toilets are. Also review any guidelines you want the Scientists to follow while they are part of **Wonder Zone**. Invite one or two Labs to the front to share their constellations.

Big bang
At the start of the session, the Professors should chat about what they like about space. Have a few facts that the Professors can try to impress each other with (choose a reputable source for your facts, such as the European Space Agency). Introduce the theme for today – the wonders of the universe. Ask the Scientists whether they have looked through binoculars or a telescope at the stars and planets.

Show the film of the session's scientist talking about what they find most amazing about the universe and discovering more about it.

Check your equipment
Invite a couple of Lab Technicians to the front to lead the club in a physical warm-up. The warm-up should be made up of simple actions that the Scientists can do safely. They should also take into consideration those who might have restricted movement.

Lab sing song
Introduce the band, the Quarks (if you're using them). Sing the **Wonder Zone** theme song, together with any actions that you have come up with. Add in another song about creation, the universe and all the different things God has made. You could sing 'Great big God' from the *Great Big God* CD or 'God made you and me' from the *Light for Everyone* CD and available from the **Wonder Zone** multimedia downloads area.

THE EXPERIMENTS

Lab practice

Introduce Lab practice, a time when you can all get exploring! This session is all about the wonders of the universe. Show the immersive video of the creation of the universe (link available in the **Wonder Zone** downloads area) and then create your own universe in a giant tub!

Fill a giant tub full of water and place in a position so that everyone can see inside it (if you're meeting in a room with a delicate floor, then you might want to do this outside). Use a paddle or large stick to stir the water around the tub to create a kind of whirlpool. Throw a handful of coarse ground pepper into the water and watch as the spin of the water sends the pepper to the centre of the tub. (You may need to give the water another stir to keep the rotation going.)

Explain that this mini-whirlpool shows something of how the solar system – the Earth, our sun and neighbouring planets – might have formed. As the sun grew in mass, gas, rock and ice started to swirl around it, the gravity pulling more material towards the centre. This is an exciting area of science that researchers are still working out; there are lots of good ideas of how it all might have happened.

Large Hadron Collider

Remind the Scientists about feeding their comments, questions pictures and jokes into the Large Hadron Collider. Read out some of the contributions that have already been put into the Collider and encourage Scientists to keep them coming!

Exploring the evidence

The Professors introduce the evidence from the Bible about God's creativity, the wonders of the universe and our own place it in!

Each day three options are suggested for telling the Bible story. You can use the same approach each time, mix and match how you tell the story or combine one of the storytelling options with the film. This repetition will help the children start to think around the story and come to some conclusions.

1. The Professors help the children to explore the passage using one of the Explore ideas below.
2. The Professors retell Psalm 8, using their own words and personal storytelling style.
3. The Professors introduce today's video storytelling episode, available to download from the **Wonder Zone** multimedia downloads area. (If you are using option 1 or 2 together with the video, then tell the story first so that the children already have the outline of events before they watch the episode.)

If you're using one of the following Explore ideas, choose the one that is most appropriate for your club. Both will help to illustrate Psalm 8 as you read the words together, as well as spark the children's wonder, creativity and imagination.

Explore 1
Give out copies of Psalm 8 from page 88 to each of the Labs and challenge them to come up with some signs and actions to go with some of the words in the psalm. For example, they might mime putting a crown on their head for the word 'ruler' (verse 1) or flap their arms for the word 'birds' (verse 8). As the Labs are working on their actions, circulate around your space and pick out one or two actions from each Lab to create a set of actions and signs for the whole club. You don't need too many, but make sure you include at least one sign or action from each Lab.

Once everyone has finished, invite some Scientists from each Lab to come to the front and demonstrate their signs. Show the words to Psalm 8 on screen and read them as the volunteers do their own signs and actions.

Then, teach your combined version to the Scientists so that you can all say the words of the psalm together as everyone does the same signs and actions.

Explore 2
Alternatively, you could encourage each of the Labs to create a prop to illustrate Psalm 8 – they could do this during Lab Prep at the start of your time together or, if you have lots of time, during your storytelling time. Give the Labs a selection of junk (various items of cardboard, plastic bottles, tin foil, bubble wrap etc) to create a given thing mentioned in Psalm 8. For example, a Lab might work together to make a large fortress (verse 2) or each Scientist might make their own sheep (verse 7).

Then, as you read out the words together, each Lab should wave their prop in the air when it is mentioned. If you don't have a large number of Scientists, you could supplement the props with

2 ● THE WONDERS OF THE UNIVERSE

some ready-made items (such as dolls or blow-up globes). Give these out to Scientists who don't have anything of their own to wave.

When you have finished, encourage the Scientists to bring their props forward to put on the stage, so that you can remember everything talked about in Psalm 8 during the rest of the session.

Observations

After the Bible exploration, the Professors should wonder about the story, focusing on these points:

- The universe is vast and amazing! It can sometimes be mind-boggling to try and think about it all!
- God created this amazing universe. He is powerful, creative and also mind-boggling.
- It is exciting to think that this same God who created the universe also cares about us. We may not seem important or as amazing as Saturn, the Milky Way or the Horsehead Nebula, but God knows us and loves us.
- He loves us so much, in fact, that he sent Jesus. The Professors should tell the children what Jesus means to them, referring to John 3:16.

The Professors should share their favourite aspects of astronomy or astrophysics, then send all the Scientists back to their Labs to put everything under the microscope!

Under the microscope

25 minutes in small groups

The canteen

The Researchers and Lab Technicians should make sure all the Scientists have made it back to the correct Labs. Hand round the refreshments and chat about what the children have discovered so far.

Test your findings: Bible exploration

With older children (8 to 11s)
Get out the star map used in Lab prep and ask the children to come up with any space facts they know. Turn to pages 12 and 13 of *Lab Book* and encourage the Scientists to fill in the names of the planets on the solar system map. (Remember that Pluto was reclassified as a dwarf planet in 2006!) Talk about how discoveries are still being made, even this close to Earth. Some astronomers and astrophysicists think there is a ninth planet beyond Neptune. No one has seen it yet, but they have seen some asteroids behaving strangely at the edge of the solar system and think that this behaviour could be caused by a rocky planet about ten times the size of Earth!

Read Psalm 8 out to the group and, as you read, encourage the children to draw, doodle or write things around the text (either on pages 14 and 15 of *Lab Book*,

THE EXPERIMENTS

or on a print-out of the words available from the **Wonder Zone** multimedia downloads area). They should draw things inspired by the words of the psalm. Give the Scientists time to colour their pictures or illuminate what they have written. Once everyone has finished, invite the children to share what they have written and drawn.

Use the mind map on page 16 to help the children process their thoughts and questions. Give the Lab a couple of minutes to jot down what they want to record about this session (if you have reluctant writers, assign a Lab Technician to help or encourage them to draw what they want to say).

Use the Scientists' questions as the basis for a discussion. Ask one of your fellow Researchers or Lab Technicians to tell the group what verses 3 and 4 mean to them. (If they can link that in with the love God showed his people by sending Jesus to live with them and die for us all, it would be good to do so.)

With younger children (5 to 8s)
Do the matching activity on page 9 of *Fact File*. Depending on the age of your children, you might want to show the children pictures of the planets before you start, so they have some idea of which is which. Chat about whether the children know anything else about the solar system.

Read Psalm 8 to the Scientists and ask them to imagine all the different things the writer talks about. They could even lie down and close their eyes as you read. Afterwards, on pages 10 and 11, encourage the Scientists to fill the space around the psalm with pictures that illustrate the passage. You might have to read parts out again so the children can remember what has been described. Chat about which part of the psalm the children like best. What does this psalm tell them about God?

Go on to record some of these ideas by helping the children to answer the questions on page 12. Encourage the children to lead this and try not to put ideas in their heads! Even children with no church background will be able to connect with something other than themselves, something bigger and ineffable.

Time to wonder
Make your space as dark as you can and give each Scientist a torch or glow stick. Ask them to switch the torches on or activate the glow sticks. Shine the lights like stars in the sky (be careful not to shine torches in people's faces). If you can, move further and further away from each other, to give the impression of the distance between stars. As you shine the lights, encourage the Scientists to give thanks to God for the vastness of the universe. Finish by thanking God for knowing and loving us (you could do this, or ask the Scientists to pray out loud, according to your Lab).

Get exploring!
20 minutes in different activities

Hands on
Choose one or more of the experiments on pages 64 and 65 for the Scientists to do. 'DIY solar system' is the most suitable, but select whichever you have the resources and space for. Enjoy discovering new things!

Construction
Show the Scientists your art and craft materials and encourage them to create whatever they like. Alternatively, choose one of the construction ideas from pages 70 to 72; 'Space and stars' is the most suitable, but select whichever you have the resources and space for.

Games
Choose one or more of the games from pages 73 to 76 to play; 'Solar system target bowls' and 'Black hole' are the most suitable, but select whichever you have the resources and space for.

Scientists' staff room
Ask a few Researchers and Lab Technicians to be in your Time Out area, so that any Scientists who would like to hang out and chat have the chance to do so.

Encourage the children to keep on discovering during this time by providing the *Book of Wonders*, open at pages 16 to 25, and copies of the *Book of Wonders: Activity Book*.

Check your results
20 minutes all together

Call all the Scientists back together and sing the **Wonder Zone** song. Read out any jokes or questions that Scientists have put into the Large Hadron Collider.

A scientist's view
Show the film of the session's scientist describing their awe and wonder at the universe, and at the fact that God loves and cares for them. Alternatively, ask a Researcher or Lab Technician to come to the front and talk about what they think about God loving them so much he sent Jesus. (Go through what they are going to say before the session, so that they are confident and happy, and you're sure that it will be suitable for the children in your club.)

The appliance of science
Devise another quiz with questions about what has happened at **Wonder Zone** today – include events at the club as well as questions about the Bible story and experiments, and some physical challenges too. Play in Labs or split the Scientists into two, playing one side of your space against the other. Make it light-hearted and not too competitive!

Drama: Discovery Team
Introduce the drama. Today the Discovery team are sent into space to investigate Saturn, but get knocked off course. Suddenly they can see the wonders of the solar system!

The knowledge
Before the session, blow up eight large balloons and stick the words of the *Learn and remember* verse to them. Split the verse up like this, sticking each section to a different balloon:

'I praise / you because of the wonderful way / you created me. / Everything you do / is marvellous! / Of this I have / no doubt.' /
Psalm 139:14 (CEV)

Ask for eight volunteers to come up to the front and hold the balloons. Encourage the other Scientists to put the volunteers/balloons in the right order to create a Bible verse solar system! Say the verse together and then either remove or pop one of the balloons (be aware that some children will be frightened by popping balloons). Say the verse again, including the missing part, and then remove or pop another balloon. Keep going until all your balloon planets have gone.

Put your heads together
Continue the balloon theme by telling the Scientists that you're going to release lots of balloons over their heads to represent planets and stars. Challenge the Scientists to bat a balloon back into the air and shout a thank you to God – either for what he has made, for the universe and our planet, or for loving us and sending us Jesus. Keep this going for a few minutes and play some lively music as the children pray.

If you can, use light-up or glow-in-the-dark balloons and turn the lights down for a starry effect!

Conclusions
Review the day's findings with the Scientists. Chat about the wonders and vastness of space, and about how God, who made the universe, made us and loves us.

Final findings
10 minutes in small groups

Chat with the Scientists about what you explored earlier in your Lab. As the Scientists wait to be collected, they can complete any unfinished pages from their *Lab Books* or *Fact Files*. Alternatively, you could work on any unfinished construction projects or revisit your experiments. Make sure everyone knows the next time you'll be meeting together. Say goodbye to each Scientist by name as they leave.

Decon chamber

It may be that some of the team have their own children at **Wonder Zone** and are unable to stay for long when the programme ends. Try to call everyone together to check any problems, briefly reminding them of the next session's activities and pray for the Holy Spirit to be at work in the children.

If you have time and the facilities, the team could share lunch together to round off the day.

THE EXPERIMENTS

EXPERIMENT 3

The colours of the rainbow

Research notes

Bible passage
John 9:1–34; 8:12

Aim
To discover more about light, both scientifically and what Jesus meant when he called himself the 'light for the world'.

Experiment summary
This session focuses on the effect of the sun on our world – bringing life to the world, light and colour to our lives and helping us to see the beauty around us. In this Bible passage, Jesus repeats his earlier statement that he is the light for the world (see John 8:12). As the children explore light and colour, this story helps them to bridge the conceptual gap to discover something of what Jesus was talking about when he said he is the 'light for the world'.

Background

Children with no church background
Children will be familiar with light and dark, and the difficulty of moving around without light. However, the concept leap needed to see that living in metaphorical darkness is also a problem might confuse some. Helping children explore the story will enable them to address this idea more clearly in their minds.

Church children
Most will be familiar with the idea that Jesus is the 'light for the world', but may never have thought further about it. Challenge church children to consider what this means for themselves. Use ideas of how life struggles without light to make the comparison. How do they live their lives in the light of Jesus?

Children of other faiths
Light is a feature of many faiths, but the claim that Jesus makes, that he is the 'light for the world', may be a surprise to children of other faiths. Wonder with the children what Jesus might be saying about himself. Resist the temptation to explain everything, allowing children to come to their own conclusions. If necessary, throw back any 'unusual' ideas or suggestions to the group and be ready to explain what you believe.

Children with additional needs
Stories of Jesus healing people often bring up difficult questions for children who have additional needs. They may struggle with being different or not being able to do everything their peers do, and wonder why Jesus doesn't make them 'better' or the same as everyone else. As you explore the story, acknowledge their frustrations, but bring them back to why Jesus healed the man and assure them that Jesus loves them.

3 • THE COLOURS OF THE RAINBOW

Doing your research

If you have done the first two sessions of **Wonder Zone**, invite the team to share some stories of what has happened so far. Thank God for all that he is already doing and then go on to explore this session's Bible story together.

Split the team into five groups and give each group a character from the story: the disciples, the blind man, the neighbours (and generally the crowd), the parents, the Pharisees. Read all of John 9 and ask the groups to look out for their given character. They should decide what motivates their character at various points in the story, and discuss why they say and do what they say and do.

Come back together and discuss the story from the different perspectives. You could do this either by asking each group in turn to share what their character goes through, or by going through the story again, frequently stopping and exploring where all the characters are at that point.

Then ask the whole group these questions:

- What is the role of 'light' in this story, both physically and metaphorically?
- What does Jesus mean in his statement in John 8:12?
- How have you experienced Jesus as 'light for the world'?
- What does this mean for the children who come to **Wonder Zone**?

Spend some time in Labs, praying for the Scientists in your small groups. Ask God to help the children to uncover something of the 'light for the world' and what that means to them. Finally, sing one or two of the songs you'll be singing in the session itself.

Then, send the team off to do the practical preparation needed for today's session.

What-you-need

- **Research kit**: items from the list on page 18
- **Lab prep**: large sheets of paper
- **Big bang**: plants and flowers, a plant that has been growing in the dark for a while
- **Lab practice**: bubble mixture, a large tub or paddling pool, a bubble wand, bubble-blowing toys, a hula hoop, swimming goggles
- **Time to wonder**: bowls of coloured sweets
- **Hands on**: items for the cress heads experiment (page 65)
- **Construction**: items for making a rainbow (page 71)
- **Games**: items for playing blindfold search or candle, tornado, room (pages 74 and 75)

The core experiment

Lab prep
10 minutes in small groups

Welcome all the Scientists to your group. Make a special welcome to any children who are new to the club today. Stand in a circle and ask each Scientist in turn to name a source of light. When a Scientist can't think of one, they have to sit down. Once you have exhausted all your ideas, congratulate the last Scientist standing and the whole group for their knowledge about light!

With a large sheet of paper and some felt-tip pens, discuss different sources of light (including the ones from the game) and write or draw them on your paper, creating a mind map. Decorate your Lab's mind map and then stick it up in your Lab area.

Have the *Book of Wonders* available, open at pages 38 and 39, and encourage the Scientists to begin to explore today's topic for themselves.

Let's investigate!
45 minutes all together

Once all the Scientists and the team are settled, the Professors should introduce themselves and welcome everyone back to **Wonder Zone**. Remind everyone about the toilets, what to do in case of a fire and the guidelines the Scientists should follow at **Wonder Zone**. Invite the Scientists to shout out all the different sources of light they came up with in their Labs.

Big bang
At the start of the session the Professors should chat about what they like about light – they should have some light facts to hand to try to impress the Scientists! Introduce the theme for today – the colours of the rainbow. It's all about light and its effects, including rainbows, why the sky is blue, how plants grow and why life needs light to survive. If possible, fill the stage with plants and flowers, including a plant that has been growing in darkness for a while. Compare this with the other, healthier-looking plants. Comment that these plants need light to grow big and strong. And the same is true for us too!

Show the film of the session's scientist talking about why studying light fascinates them, what first attracted them to it and the most amazing discovery they have made.

Check your equipment
Invite a couple of Lab Technicians to the front to lead the club in a physical warm-up. The warm-up should be made up of simple actions that the Scientists can do safely. They should also take into consideration those who might have restricted movement.

Lab sing song
Reintroduce the band, the Quarks (if you're using them). Sing the **Wonder Zone** theme song, together with your actions. Introduce a new song, perhaps one about light. You could use the song 'Follow me', available at the **Wonder Zone** multimedia downloads area.

Lab practice
Introduce Lab practice, a time when you can all get exploring! Today's scientific experiment is all about creating giant bubbles. In addition to being a fun introduction to the session, it helps children to explore refraction and understand how rainbows occur!

Before the session, make up a large amount of bubble mixture, using the fact sheet available at the **Wonder Zone** multimedia downloads area. If possible, do this experiment outside. (You can do it inside, but make sure you cover the floor using waterproof mats or tablecloths.)

Pour the bubble mixture into a large tub or small paddling pool – if possible, it should be big enough for a child to stand in. Use a bubble wand (the kind you get in a tube of bubble mixture) to blow some bubbles. Point out how you can see all the colours of the rainbow on the surface of each bubble.

Use different ways of blowing a bubble (various toys are available online, or your team may already have some). Finally use a hula hoop – lay it flat in the paddling pool/tub and lift it directly upwards. You should end up with a bubble tube! Invite a Scientist to take their shoes and socks off and stand in the pool/tub. (If they have sensitive skin, provide a clean pair of wellington boots for them to wear. You could also give them some swimming goggles or safety glasses to protect their eyes.) Lift up the hula hoop – the Scientist should be inside the bubble tube!

Once you have cleaned up the mess (or gone inside), explain the scientific background to the experiment. Sunlight is made up of lots of different colours. Most of the time they are all mixed up so we don't see them separately, but sometimes they get split up and that's when we see rainbows.

Usually, this happens when the light gets bent (this is called refraction) by things like water (you can see this happening when you look at a straw in a glass of water). Different colours in the light get bent by different amounts, so sometimes this lets us see a rainbow. This is how rainbows happen in the sky: the light is refracted (bent) by water droplets in the atmosphere into the colours of the rainbow.

Rainbows on bubbles happen a little differently. Bubbles are made of a really thin layer of water trapped between two really thin layers of soap. Sunlight is reflected (bounced) off the outside surface of the bubble, but also off the inside surface of the bubble. These are a tiny distance apart so our eyes see two different reflections of the light, a tiny bit apart. These are so close together that they mess around with each other. Some bits of the light add together, making some colours brighter, and others cancel out. That means that the light gets split up and we see some of the rainbow colours in the bubble.

Large Hadron Collider

Remind the Scientists that they can feed their comments, questions, pictures and jokes into the Large Hadron Collider. Encourage everyone to put something into the Collider today! Show some of the things that have already been put into the Collider and thank those whose contributions you have shared.

Exploring the evidence

The Professors introduce the evidence from the Bible about the power of light! Challenge the Scientists to observe what happens and see how light plays a part in this story.

Each day three options are suggested for telling the Bible story. You can use the same approach each time, mix and match how you tell the story or combine the storytelling script (or your own retelling) with the film. This repetition will help the children start to think around the story and come to some conclusions.

1 The Professors retell the story using the script on page 60. Today, the interview is with a blind man called Ben; make sure you have rehearsed it before the session.

2 The Professors tell the story from John 9, using their own words and personal storytelling style.

3 The Professors introduce today's video storytelling episode, available to download from the **Wonder Zone** multimedia downloads area. (If you are using option 1 or 2 together with the video, then tell the story first so that the children already have the outline of events before they watch the episode.)

Observations

After the story, the Professors should wonder about the story, focusing on these points:

- Jesus gave sight to a man who couldn't see. He literally gave light to him.

- Through this miracle, Jesus talked about being 'spiritually' blind as well as being 'literally' blind. He meant that the religious leaders – the people who were in charge – were focusing on all the wrong

THE EXPERIMENTS

things. They had made up lots of rules that everyone had to follow. They wanted to make sure everyone kept those rules, but they couldn't see that Jesus was more important than any of those! He called them blind, but he didn't mean literally. He meant they were missing the most important thing – him!

- Jesus said that he is 'light for the world'. In John 8:12, he says he is the light that gives life. The light of the sun gives physical life to plants, animals and us, Jesus gives us spiritual life.
- We don't have to live in darkness, where we're messed up by the things we do wrong and are tripped up by our mistakes. We can live in the light, which gives us freedom!

The Professors then send the Scientists off to their Labs to explore the story further.

Under the microscope

25 minutes in small groups

The canteen

The Researchers and Lab Technicians should make sure all the Scientists have made it back to the correct Labs. Hand round the refreshments and chat about what the children have discovered so far.

Test your findings: Bible exploration

With older children (8 to 11s)

Turn to page 18 of *Lab Book* and colour in the rainbow. As you do so, chat about when rainbows occur and ask if anyone knows why they happen. Sunlight (or white light) is made up of lots of different colours all mixed up. When they're mixed up they look white or see-through. When light hits a drop of rain (or water spray) the water reflects the light, refracts it (changes its direction) and disperses it (splits it up into its different wavelengths), and so we see the different colours in the order red, orange, yellow, green, blue, indigo and violet. (If you wish, you could make a large rainbow and stick it up in your Lab.)

On page 19, do the spot the difference puzzle and then think about the differences between the two plants. The pale and spindly plant hasn't had enough light. Light gives life to plants. Plants use chlorophyll (the substance that makes them green) to turn light and carbon dioxide into food. If there isn't any light, the plant puts all its effort into growing so that it can get to some light!

Go on to read the story on pages 20 and 21. At each pause in the story, ask the group how the characters might be feeling. Draw in suitable facial expressions on the blank faces. Chat about the Scientists' initial reactions to the story. What do they think the religious leaders thought of Jesus? Get some ideas and try to draw out any reasons why this might be the case. Go on to wonder why they were horrible to the man who was blind.

Turn to page 22 and encourage the Lab to draw or write their ideas about what Jesus meant when he said he was 'light for the world'. Draw some parallels back to plants and light.

With younger children (5 to 8s)

Use felt-tip pens, crayons or squares of coloured paper and glue sticks to fill in the blank rainbow on page 13 of *Fact File*. As you work, chat together about what the children think when they see a rainbow. You could briefly share the story of Noah as a way of explaining what it means to Christians.

Read the first part of today's story from page 14 (or read John 9:1–7 from a Bible – the Contemporary English Version is used in *Fact File*) and chat about what is happening. Ask the Scientists how the blind man might feel now he can see. Fill in a suitable expression on the blank face.

Read out the summary of the rest of the story from page 15. Review the whole story and then ask the children what they think about Jesus. Who is he? Why did he make the man see? The Scientists will probably have lots of questions, and not all of them will seem relevant. However, some of these strange questions will be the result of children thinking through what you have discovered together and trying to make sense of it in the context of their life experience.

Following on from this, give the Scientists space to fill in their answer to the question on page 16. If any children are struggling, then chat about it with them, but help them come to their own conclusions, rather than giving them an answer.

Time to wonder

Place a bowl of sweets in the centre of the group. Make sure you have some or all of the colours of the rainbow in the sweet bowl (indigo sweets might be hard to come by, so we haven't included a suggestion for that). Take it in turns to take a sweet and pray a prayer linked to the colour:

- **Red**: talk to God about what you have discovered today
- **Orange**: ask God for something you need
- **Yellow**: tell God how amazing he is
- **Green**: thank God for something he has created on land
- **Blue**: thank God for something he has created in the sea
- **Violet**: thank God for something he has created in the sky

Once each Scientist has prayed they can eat their sweet! If you have time, you can all have another turn.

Get exploring!

20 minutes in different activities

Hands on
Choose one or more of the experiments on pages 63 to 68 for the Scientists to do. 'Cress head' is the most suitable, but select whichever you have the resources and space for. Enjoy discovering new things!

Construction
Show the Scientists your art and craft materials and encourage them to create whatever they like. Alternatively, choose one of the construction ideas from pages 70 to 72; 'Rainbow' is the most suitable, but select whichever you have the resources and space for.

Games
Choose one or more of the games from pages 73 to 76 to play; 'Blindfold search' and 'Candle, tornado, room' are the most suitable, but select whichever you have the resources and space for.

Scientists' staff room
Ask a few Researchers and Lab Technicians to be in your Time Out area, so that any Scientists who would like to hang out and chat have the chance to do so.

Encourage the children to keep on discovering during this time by providing the *Book of Wonders*, open at pages 38 and 39, and copies of the *Book of Wonders: Activity Book*.

Check your results

20 minutes all together

Call all the Scientists back together and sing the **Wonder Zone** song. Read out any jokes or questions that Scientists have put into the Large Hadron Collider.

A scientist's view
Show the film of a scientist describing their fascination with the role light plays in the world, and how Jesus is light for the world. Alternatively, ask a Researcher or Lab Technician to come to the front and talk about what Jesus' light means to them. (Go through what they are going to say before the session, so that they are confident and happy, and you're sure that it will be suitable for the children in your club.)

The appliance of science
Devise another quiz with questions about what has happened at **Wonder Zone** today – include events at the club as well as questions about the Bible story and experiments, and some physical challenges too. Play in Labs or split the Scientists into two teams, playing one side of your space against the other. Make it light-hearted and not too competitive!

Drama: Discovery Team

Introduce the drama. Today, the Discovery team are sent to the Houses of Parliament to investigate some strange lights. They go via some underground tunnels, but soon lose all their lights. Can they get out of the tunnels safely?

The knowledge

Invite any Scientists who think they can remember the *Learn and remember* verse to come to the front and say the verse. Congratulate any who manage to remember the verse and help any who struggle!

Put the verse up on screen and say it all together:

'I praise you because of the wonderful way you created me. Everything you do is marvellous! Of this I have no doubt.'
Psalm 139:14 (CEV)

Put your heads together

Explain that you're going to pray an action prayer together. Encourage all the children to crouch down low and say this prayer:

Thank you, God, for giving us light for us to grow. (All pretend to grow like plants.)

Thank you that we can grow big and strong! (Flex muscles.)

Thank you, Jesus, for being the 'light for the world', helping us discover how to live. (All point in different directions.)

Help us to discover more about what it means to be your friend. (Shake hands with the person next to you.)

Finish by all shouting, **'Amen!'**

Conclusion

Review the day's findings with the Scientists. Chat about light, its nature and how it helps us to grow healthy and strong. Remind them about the ideas everyone came up with about what Jesus being 'light for the world' means. Then send everyone back to their Labs to be collected by their parents or carers.

Final findings

10 minutes in small groups

Chat with the Scientists about what you explored earlier in your Lab. As the Scientists wait to be collected, they can complete any unfinished pages from their *Lab Books* or *Fact Files*. Alternatively, you could work on any unfinished construction projects or revisit your experiments. Make sure everyone knows the next time you'll be meeting together. Say goodbye to each Scientist by name as they leave.

Decon chamber

It may be that some of the team have their own children at **Wonder Zon**e and are unable to stay for long when the programme ends. Try to call everyone together to check any problems, briefly reminding them of the next session's activities and pray for the Holy Spirit to be at work in the children.

If you have time and the facilities, the team could share lunch together to round off the day.

EXPERIMENT 4

The creatures of the world

Research notes

Bible passage
Psalms 104; 139

Aim
To explore the diversity and nature of God's creation, and our place in it.

Experiment summary
Most children love animals – both the cute ones and the ones that seem really weird – and this session will help them explore the natural world and how they fit in with it. God cares about the whole world, and that includes us. What is our reaction to that, both personally and in the way we treat the world around us? Psalm 104 will help children think about the breadth of the natural world, while Psalm 139 enables children to discover that God cares for them.

Background

Children with no church background
For some children, the idea that anyone is interested in them might (sadly) be a surprise. That God has been interested in them and loved them since before they were born can be a powerful realisation. Help children to reflect on this and be affirmed that, even among such a diverse world, God cares about them.

Church children
Psalm 139 is often used in Sunday School, but help church children consider what this means to them. If God is responsible for the whole world, and for their existence, what's their response to that? Sharing testimonies about what this means might help children explore it for themselves.

Children of other faiths
That God can know children, love them individually and be interested in their lives might be surprising to children from other faiths. Leaders talking about their own relationship with God will help children get an understanding of how God loves and interacts with his people.

Children with additional needs
Psalm 139 is an encouraging and comforting psalm, but can lead children with additional needs to conclude that God purposely made them with the difficulties they struggle with day to day. Be sensitive and help children to express themselves when talking with God about this. The psalm focuses on the wonder of God knowing and loving us so intimately, in all the good and hard things in our lives, rather than being an explanation of why things are the way they are.

THE EXPERIMENTS

Doing your research

Give out sheets of paper and some art materials. Tell the team that you are going to read out Psalm 104 and they should listen and draw something that stands out to them. (You could also do this with play dough or pipe cleaners, and ask the team to model something from the psalm.)

What-you-need

- **Research kit**: items from the list on page 18

- **Lab prep**: large sheets of paper

- **Lab practice**: small animals, animal videos

- **Exploring the evidence**: printed copies of Psalm 104 (page 89), Psalm 104 PowerPoint

- **Test your findings**: bird books, emojis, face stickers

- **Time to wonder**: animal and people shapes (page 90)

- **Hands on**: items for experiments about themselves (pages 66 and 67)

- **Construction**: items for making animal prints (page 72)

- **Games**: items for playing the king of the jungle or animal obstacles (page 75)

Give people a few minutes to finish their creations, and then encourage the team to share why they drew or made what they did. Bring everyone back together and see if you can make up a visual representation of the psalm from the things the team have created. If possible, spend a few moments singing a song that talks about God's power and creativity.

Ask people to go back into their small groups and read Psalm 139 together. On another sheet of paper, ask the small groups to create a word picture of God, including words inspired by the psalm. They should try to use two different colours: one for words that describe who God is, and one for words that describe his attitude to us.

Get some feedback from the groups, asking for volunteers to show and explain their group's word picture. What do all these word pictures tell us about God? Use the word pictures as a basis for prayer, thanking God for creating the world, but loving us so much that he is interested in us, our thoughts, feelings, words and deeds. Ask the Researchers and Lab Technicians to pray for the children in their Labs, that they would catch sight of God's love today.

Then send the team off to do the practical preparation needed for today's session.

The core experiment

Lab prep
10 minutes in small groups

Welcome all the Scientists to your group. Make a special welcome to any children who are new to the club today. Conduct a survey in your group about your favourite and least favourite animals. What kinds of animals are popular and which are not? Is there a big difference in people's choices? Make a chart of all the responses on a large sheet of paper. Then send one or two Scientists to another Lab to find out the responses others have given. Welcome Scientists visiting from other Labs and share your results. When your Scientists return, add the results they have discovered to your chart.

Alternatively, have a go at creating your own animal! Put together parts from different animals to construct a new creature. Play a version of 'I went to market…' to make the new creature. For example: 'If I made an animal, it would have the ears of a dog.'; 'If I made an animal it would have the ears of a dog and the legs of a frog.' And so on.

Have the *Book of Wonders* available, open at pages 60 to 77, and encourage the Scientists to begin to explore today's topic for themselves.

Let's investigate!
45 minutes all together

Once all the Scientists and the team are settled, the Professors should introduce themselves and welcome everyone back to **Wonder Zone**. Remind everyone about the toilets, what to do in case of a fire and the guidelines the Scientists should follow at **Wonder Zone**. Invite some Scientists up to the stage to show the 'favourite animals' chart they created in Lab Prep. What came out as your club's favourite animal?

Big bang
At the start of the session the Professors should chat about what their favourite animals are and show some pictures of those animals (include some wonderfully weird ones, too!). The Professors should have some fascinating facts about those animals to amaze the Scientists! Introduce the theme for today – the creatures of the world. Comment that the world is full of diverse creatures, from fish at the bottom of the sea to birds that fly high in the sky!

Show the film of the session's scientist talking about why they study their particular specialist creature, what first attracted them to it and the most amazing discovery they have made.

Lab sing song
Introduce the Quarks (if you're using them). Sing the **Wonder Zone** theme song, together with your actions. Introduce a new song, perhaps one about God's creativity. You could use the song 'God made you and me' from the *Light for Everyone* CD, available at the **Wonder Zone** multimedia downloads area.

Lab practice
Introduce Lab practice, a time when you can all get exploring! Today's scientific experiment is all about exploring some of the creatures of the world!

If you can, ask someone who owns spiders, small reptiles or small pets (such as guinea pigs) to come and show them

THE EXPERIMENTS

to the children. Ask them to tell the Scientists about their particular animal, what they eat, where they sleep and how they keep them. (Do they need heat? Do they live in a tank or a pen?) If possible, invite some Scientists to the front to handle the animals. What do they feel like? Are they light or heavy? Do they make any noise when they move? (Make sure the welfare of the animals is kept in mind at all times and they are not subjected to stress.)

If this isn't possible, show one or two videos of amazing animals. The BBC Earth and BBC Earth Unplugged channels on YouTube are good sources of interesting videos (make sure you check the videos before the session so that you're sure they are suitable). Try to find films of animals that are unusual and surprising, such as a giant octopus or tarantula. Be amazed about the different animals!

Large Hadron Collider

Remind the Scientists that they can feed their comments, questions, pictures and jokes into the Large Hadron Collider. Encourage everyone to put something into the Collider today! Show some of the things that have already been put into the Collider and thank those whose contributions you have shared.

Exploring the evidence

The Professors introduce the evidence from the Bible about the amazing natural world, which includes us too.

Each day three options are suggested for telling the Bible story. You can use the same approach each time, mix and match how you tell the story or combine one of the storytelling options with the film. This repetition will help the children start to think around the story and come to some conclusions.

1 The Professors help the children explore the passage using the activity below.

2 The Professors tell the story from Psalm 104, using their own words and personal storytelling style.

3 The Professors introduce today's video storytelling episode, available to download from the **Wonder Zone** multimedia downloads area. (If you are using option 1 or 2 together with the video, then tell the story first so that the children already have the outline of events before they watch the episode.)

Exploration activity

Send the Scientists back to their Labs so that they can help out with today's storytelling. Make sure each of the Labs has a copy of one of these sections of Psalm 104 (available on page 89):

- Verses 1–4
- Verses 5–9
- Verses 10–15
- Verses 16–18
- Verses 19–23
- Verses 24–26

If you have fewer than six Labs, choose as many of the sections as you need. Encourage each Lab to read through their section of the psalm and create sound effects to illustrate that section. If they like, they can also do actions to accompany their sounds.

When all the Labs have created their sound effects, call everyone back together. Read out Psalm 104 and encourage the Labs to perform their noises and actions as you do so. You can accompany this with the PowerPoint presentation found in the **Wonder Zone** multimedia downloads area.

When you get to verse 33, encourage the Labs to do their sound effects all at once as a praise to God, and then all cheer!

Observations

After the story, the Professors should wonder about the story, focusing on these points:

- The world in which we live is rich and diverse with life – plants, animals and humans.
- God created this world, from the very start of everything to today. And there is so much of it – life on earth is abundant! The person who wrote the psalm praises God because of what he has done. Do we want to do the same thing?
- Even though the psalm writer didn't know everything we know now through science, they were still able to praise God for the things they saw in the world around them, and we can do the same!
- God cares for the world and wants us to care for it too. Challenge the children to think about how we look after the world in which we live.

The Professors should talk about the ways they help to look after God's world (recycling, not using plastics, planting a wildflower patch in their garden etc). They should then send the Scientists off to their Labs to explore the passage further.

Under the microscope

25 minutes in small groups

The canteen

The Researchers and Lab Technicians should make sure all the Scientists have made it back to the correct Labs. Hand round the refreshments and chat about what the children have discovered so far.

Test your findings: Bible exploration

With older children (8 to 11s)
If you can go outside (or at least look out of a window), help the Scientists to conduct the bird survey on page 26 of *Lab Book*. (This may not be possible in all situations, so suggest that children do this at home.) You might find it helpful to have a bird book or access to the RSPB website to help identify the different birds you can see. The Woodland Trust has animal ID wheels that could maybe be useful for exploration of the birds and other wildlife found in church grounds or gardens at home. (Visit www.woodlandtrust.org.uk/naturedetectives/ for ideas.) Chat about the diversity of the birds you can see. For example, pigeons, crows and sparrows are all different sizes and have different plumage.

Continue the idea of diversity by doing the picture quiz on page 27. Challenge the Scientists to spot what the animals are from just a small part of them. Which of these animals are the children's favourites?

Turn to pages 28 and 29 and read through the verses from Psalm 139. Chat about how God made the world around us, and made us too. The world is big, and we are quite small in comparison, but God cares for each one of us. Read through the verses again, this time encouraging the Scientists to draw emojis around the page to show what the verses make them feel. You might find it useful to have print-outs of some common emojis to inspire the children. If they are struggling, they can circle or copy the examples dotted around pages 28 and 29.

Share some of the emojis the children have drawn. Why did they draw them? If appropriate, share something of what these verses mean to you with the Lab. Help the Scientists put some of these ideas into the psalm on page 30. They can write or draw in the spaces of the psalm structure to create their own psalm. Be led by the children in this activity – don't try to guide them to the 'correct' answers (because there aren't any!).

With younger children (5 to 8s)
If you can, go outside and see what different creatures you can find. Look under rocks, in the sky or in bushes to see birds and minibeasts. Encourage the Scientists to draw some of them on page 17 of *Fact File*.

Read Psalm 139:1–6,13–18 to the children (from pages 18 and 19 or a Bible). As you read, ask them to think about how it makes them feel. Encourage them to decorate the pages with faces that describe how they feel (eg smiley, frowning, sad or laughing). It might help to have some stickers so that the children can choose which face they want. Once everyone has finished, compare the different emotions and try to get the children to describe why they chose those faces.

Remind the children of the *Learn and remember* verse on page 20. Chat about what it might mean.

THE EXPERIMENTS

You could even do the *Learn and remember* verse puzzle on pages 26 and 27 to help to talk about it further. You could use some of these ideas in Time to wonder.

Time to wonder

Give each Scientist a pen and an animal or person shape cut out of card (available on page 90). Have a time of quiet and encourage the children to write or draw on their animal or person shape what they want to say to God because of everything they've discovered today. It could be thanking God for all the different animals in the world, or for making them, or for caring about them. Some children may be unhappy because things have gone wrong (for example, a relative is ill or has died and God didn't seem to care). Be sensitive and help the child express their feelings without giving any 'pat' answers or advice. Sit with the child in their sadness.

Get exploring!

20 minutes in different activities

Hands on

Choose one or more of the experiments on pages 63 to 68 for the Scientists to do. 'Experiments about me' is the most suitable, but select whichever you have the resources and space for. Enjoy discovering new things!

Construction

Show the Scientists your art and craft materials and encourage them to create whatever they like. Alternatively, choose one of the construction ideas from pages 70 to 72; 'Animal printing' is the most suitable, but select whichever you have the resources and space for.

Games

Choose one or more of the games from pages 73 to 76 to play; 'The king of the jungle' and 'Animal obstacles' are the most suitable, but select whichever you have the resources and space for.

Scientists' staff room

Ask a few Researchers and Lab Technicians to be in your Time Out area, so that any Scientists who would like to hang out and chat have the chance to do so.

Encourage the children to keep on discovering during this time by providing the *Book of Wonders*, open at pages 60 to 77, and copies of the *Book of Wonders: Activity Book*.

Check your results

20 minutes all together

Call all the Scientists back together and sing the **Wonder Zone** song. Read out any jokes or questions that Scientists have put into the Large Hadron Collider.

A scientist's view

Show the film of a scientist describing their excitement about the diversity of the natural world and how God fits into that for them. Alternatively, ask a Researcher or Lab Technician to come to the front and talk about what creation means to them, and how they feel about God creating, knowing and loving them. (Go through what they are going to say before the session, so that they are confident and happy, and you're sure that it will be suitable for the children in your club.)

The appliance of science

Devise another quiz with questions about what has happened at **Wonder Zone** today – include events at the club as well as questions about the Bible story and experiments, and some physical challenges too. Play in Labs or split the Scientists into two teams, playing one side of your space against the other. Make it light-hearted and not too competitive!

Drama: Discovery Team

Introduce the drama. The Discovery team gets miniaturised to investigate the ants that are swarming all over the lab.

The knowledge

Put your *Learn and remember* verse up on screen and say it all together:

'I praise you because of the wonderful way you created me. Everything you do is marvellous! Of this I have no doubt.'
Psalm 139:14 (CEV)

Tell the Scientists that a caterpillar has got into the system and is gradually eating the words of the verse. Remove a few words and then ask the club to say the whole verse. Continue until all the words have been 'eaten'. (If you have talented artists in your team, you could get them to write out the verse on large sheets of paper and make a large caterpillar. As the caterpillar eats the words, tear them out of the paper. At the end, you should just be left with shreds!)

Put your heads together

Say this prayer and invite the Scientists to join in at the appropriate points:

Thank you, God, for all the great animals that are on land!

Ask the Scientists to do sounds and actions of their favourite land animal.

Thank you, God, for all the great animals that live in the sea!

Ask the Scientists to do sounds and actions of their favourite sea creature.

Thank you, God, for all the great animals that fly in the air!

Ask the Scientists to do sounds and actions of their favourite flying animal.

Thank you, God, for making me!

Ask the Scientists to do join hands and shout '**hurray**'!

Conclusions

Review the day's findings with the Scientists. Chat about the diversity of God's creation and about how God, who made all these creatures and plants, made us and loves us. Send everyone back to their Labs to be collected by their parents or carers.

Final findings

10 minutes in small groups

Chat with the Scientists about what you explored earlier in your Lab. As the Scientists wait to be collected, they can complete any unfinished pages from their *Lab Books* or *Fact Files*. Alternatively, you could work on any unfinished construction projects or revisit your experiments.

Decon chamber

It may be that some of the team have their own children at **Wonder Zone** and are unable to stay for long when the programme ends. Try to call everyone together to check any problems, briefly reminding them of the next session's activities and pray for the Holy Spirit to be at work in the children.

If you have time and the facilities, the team could share lunch together to round off the day.

EXPERIMENT 5: The possibilities of robots

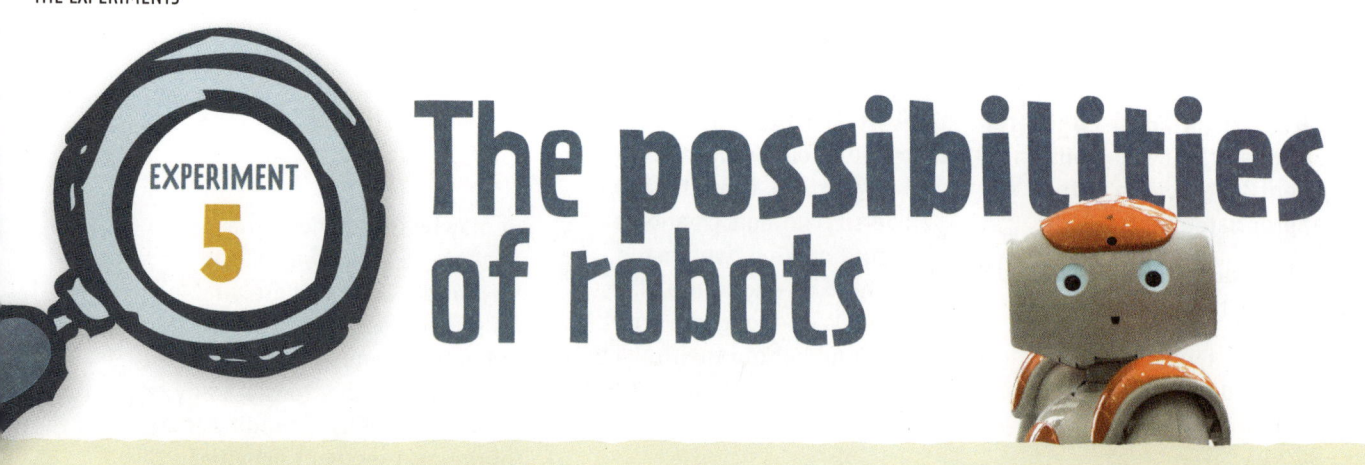

Research notes

Bible passage
Luke 15:11–32

Aim
To discover that we have the ability to choose what we do – and to choose Jesus.

Experiment summary
Children will have encountered robots and AI, from the simple robots you can buy in the shops to those they have discovered about at school – complex ones that can learn from experience and better follow their programming. Yet, can even the most sophisticated AI choose what they do, or must they always follow their programming? Through the familiar story of the lost son, the children will think about our ability to choose to follow Jesus or not, and what that might mean for us.

Background

Children with no church background
The story of the lost son will likely resonate strongly with those who have never heard it before. The forgiveness the father shows can be eye-opening. Tell children that that same forgiveness is open to them. All they have to do is choose to be God's friend. Remain sensitive to the fact that all children may have differing/difficult experiences of fathers.

Church children
Over-familiarity might well breed contempt for children who might have heard this story several times. Help the children play with this story, to see themselves in different places – would they have done what the father did? Or the younger son? Do they feel like the older son? How did it feel for the younger son to be forgiven? Remain sensitive to the fact that all children may have differing/difficult experiences of fathers.

Children of other faiths
It is important to be aware of what asking children of other faiths to choose Jesus means. Of course, we want everyone to know Jesus and follow him, but there will be consequences with families if a child from another faith makes that choice. Always be sensitive and keep children's family situations in mind. Remain sensitive to the fact that all children may have differing/difficult experiences of fathers.

Children with additional needs
The kind of unconditional acceptance and love shown by the father to his returning son may not be the universal experience of children with additional needs. The reality of many is of difficulties in relationships caused by their needs. It is important to mirror this love and understanding in everything we do, encouraging all children to be accepting of each other. Remain sensitive to the fact that all children may have differing/difficult experiences of fathers.

Doing your research

Ask the team to reflect on all the robots and AI that play a part in their life. What kinds of things help them? Then ask them to consider the differences and similarities between humans and robots/AI. Break into small groups to do this, and then get some feedback once everyone has finished.

Get some feedback from the groups about the different decisions and the reasons behind them. Then go on to discuss these questions:

- What was family life like for these three before the story starts?
- What might have happened in that family after the end of the story?
- Do you identify with anyone in the story? Who and why?
- What are the most important choices that we can make?
- When you chose to follow Jesus, what was it like?

Back in smaller groups, ask everyone to read the story of the lost son from Luke 15:11–32. As they do so, encourage them to make a list of all the decisions taken in the story. Remind them to include decisions taken not to do something as well as decisions about taking action. Once they have finished, ask the groups to reflect on why the characters decided to do (or not to do) something.

This is the last session of **Wonder Zone** (if you're doing the Experiments in order), but remind your team not to wind down! Ask Researchers and Lab Technicians to get together and pray for the Scientists in their Labs. Pray that they will have an amazing time and that they will discover the choice they can make to follow Jesus.

What-you-need

- **Research kit**: items from the list on page 18
- **Lab prep**: simple robots (see text for details)
- **Lab practice**: robots, large sheets of paper, internet access (optional)
- **Test your findings**: large sheets of paper
- **Time to wonder**: copies of *What Do You Believe?* and *What is Being a Christian All About?*
- **Hands on**: items for the power of instructions experiment (page 68)
- **Construction**: items for making moving figures (page 72)
- **Games**: items for playing if you love me… or grand prix (page 76)
- **Put your heads together**: sign language video

Then send the team off to do the practical preparation needed for today's session.

THE EXPERIMENTS

The core experiment

⏰ Lab prep
10 minutes in small groups

Welcome all the Scientists to your group. Make a special welcome to any children who are new to the club today. Show the children a simple robot, such as a robotic dog or other robot toy (these are available cheaply in toy shops or online – or people in your congregation might be able to lend them to you). Play with the robot and explore what it can (and can't) do. Ask the children to imitate the robot and do some daily activities as if they were a robot. You could do this all together or see who is the best robot in your Lab!

Have the *Book of Wonders* available, open at pages 104 and 105, and encourage the Scientists to begin to explore today's topic for themselves.

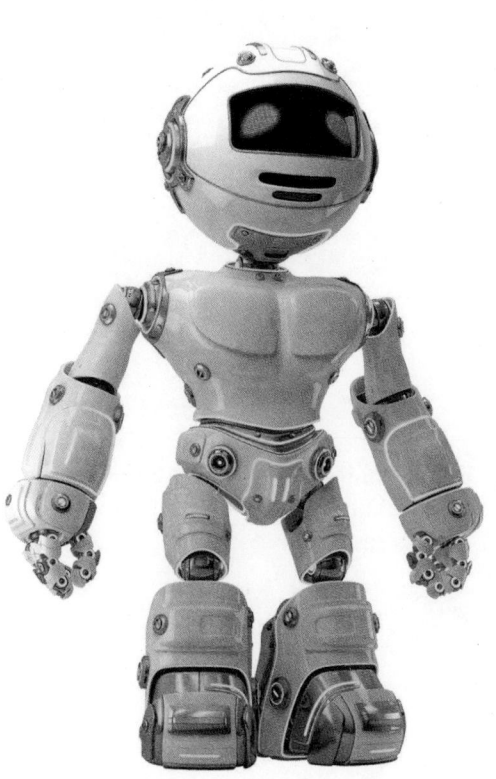

🔍 Let's investigate!
45 minutes all together

Once all the Scientists and the team are settled, the Professors should introduce themselves and welcome everyone back to **Wonder Zone**. Remind everyone about the toilets, what to do in case of a fire and the guidelines the Scientists should follow at **Wonder Zone**. Invite some Scientists up to the stage to showcase the robot impressions they created during Lab prep.

Big bang
At the start of the session the Professors should chat about what robots they have experience of – these could include robot vacuum cleaners or robots they work with as part of their job. Introduce the theme for today – the possibilities of robots. Ask the Scientists what amazing robots they have seen. They may have built simple robots at school.

Show the film of the session's scientist talking about what they love about robotics, the development of AI and how robots play a big part in daily life.

Check your equipment
Invite a couple of Lab Technicians to the front to lead the club in a physical warm-up. The warm-up should be made up of simple actions that the Scientists can do safely. They should also take into consideration those who might have restricted movement.

Lab sing song
Introduce the Quarks again (if you're using them). Sing the **Wonder Zone** theme song, together with your actions. Sing one or two of the songs that you have already sung at **Wonder Zone**.

Lab practice
Introduce Lab practice, a time when you can all get exploring! There are two options, depending on what you have available. If you have access to a larger robot (larger than the ones the Scientists looked at in Lab prep), show it to the club now and show the children what it can do. If possible, invite some volunteers to the front to interact with the robot. What tricks can it do? On a large sheet of paper, record what it can and can't do. (If you can't get hold of a robot, show some videos of robots in action. Show the Scientists the first frame of the film and ask them to guess what the robot can do.) Comment that, at the moment, robots can't make the same kind of choices that we can. Isn't it interesting that we might see them be able to do things more like us one day?

Alternatively, if there is suitable access to the internet, set up a voice assistant, such as Siri, Alexa or Cortana. Together, come up with a variety of questions for the assistant to answer (weeding out any inappropriate questions as you go!). Again, as with the robot experiment, on a large sheet of paper, keep a record of which questions it can and can't help you with. Make sure your security settings are at the correct level, so that the assistant doesn't suggest anything inappropriate!

If any of the team has used the AI app Replika (a chatbot that learns your personality as you talk to it), invite them to the front to talk about it. Is the chatbot a friend?

Large Hadron Collider

Remind the Scientists that they can feed their comments, questions, pictures and jokes into the Large Hadron Collider. Encourage everyone to put something into the Collider today before it's too late! Show some of the things that have already been put into the Collider and thank those whose contributions you have shared.

Exploring the evidence

The Professors introduce the evidence from the Bible about making good and bad choices, and how we can choose to be God's friend.

Each day three options are suggested for telling the Bible story. You can use the same approach each time, mix and match how you tell the story or combine the storytelling script (or your own retelling) with the film. This repetition will help the children start to think around the story and come to some conclusions.

1 The Professor retells the story using the script on pages 61 and 62. Today, the interview is with the younger son (called Judah here); make sure you have rehearsed it before the session.

2 The Professor tells the story from Luke 15:11–32, using their own words and personal storytelling style.

3 The Professor introduces today's video storytelling episode, available to download from the **Wonder Zone** multimedia downloads area. (If you are using option 1 or 2 together with the video, then tell the story first so that the children already have the outline of events before they watch the episode.)

Observations

After the story, the Professors should wonder about the story, focusing on these points:

- Robots, computers and artificial intelligence are amazing: they can do many things we can't, in places we can't go (under water, in space, at extreme temperatures). Sometimes robots can seem very similar to us and do the same things as we do.

- Yet, today's robots, computers and artificial intelligence are not able to make emotional choices. They might be good at playing your favourite music for you, but they can't choose to be someone's friend. They don't make decisions that aren't good for them. But we do sometimes.

THE EXPERIMENTS

- The younger son in the story made bad choices at the start. He made the rest of his family sad, he was selfish and he wasted his money. However, he realised his mistakes and returned home to say sorry. His dad was waiting for his son to come home, and forgave him!

- Like the younger son, we can make some bad choices. But these things don't stop us from being God's friend. Just as the father in the story welcomed his son back, God loves us and wants to welcome us into his family. He offers us the chance to wipe the slate clean and start again!

The Professors could talk about the robots that amaze them before sending the Scientists off to their Labs to explore the story further.

Under the microscope

25 minutes in small groups

The canteen

The Researchers and Lab Technicians should make sure all the Scientists have made it back to the correct Labs. Hand round the refreshments and chat about what the children have discovered so far.

Test your findings: Bible exploration

With older children (8 to 11s)
Turn to page 32 of *Lab Book* and encourage the Scientists to design a robot in the space provided. Alternatively, they could do this on large sheets of paper and stick them up in the Lab. Compare the different robots and ask the Scientists to describe what they do.

Go on to think about the dilemmas on page 33. Don't judge what the children say, or tell them there is a 'right' answer. Focus more on how they make their choices. What bases do they use to decide what to do? Have the children ever been in these kinds of situations?

Read the story of the lost son together, stopping at the points indicated on pages 34 and 35 of *Lab Book* and answering the questions. Chat about why Jesus told this story. He was trying to show the religious leaders of the day that he had come to rescue those people who were lost, like the son in the story. God's love is for everyone, not just people who are 'good' or who 'deserve' it. The younger son had made a mess of his life. He realised he had to go home and start again. We too can choose to follow Jesus, even if we feel we've made a mess of things. Use the space on page 36 to help the children process their reactions to the story.

Ask the Scientists:

- What do you think about this story? How does it make you feel?
- What do you want to do now you have explored this story?

With younger children (5 to 8s)
Read out some of the questions on page 21 of *Fact File* and ask the children what choices they would make if they were in those situations.

Read the first part of the story from page 22 (or read Luke 15:11–21 from a Bible). Ask the children what they think happened next. What do they think about what the younger son did? Do they think the father will accept him back? Go on to read the second part from page 23 (or read Luke 15:22–32). Were the children right in what they thought would happen? Ask if they are surprised about what happened.

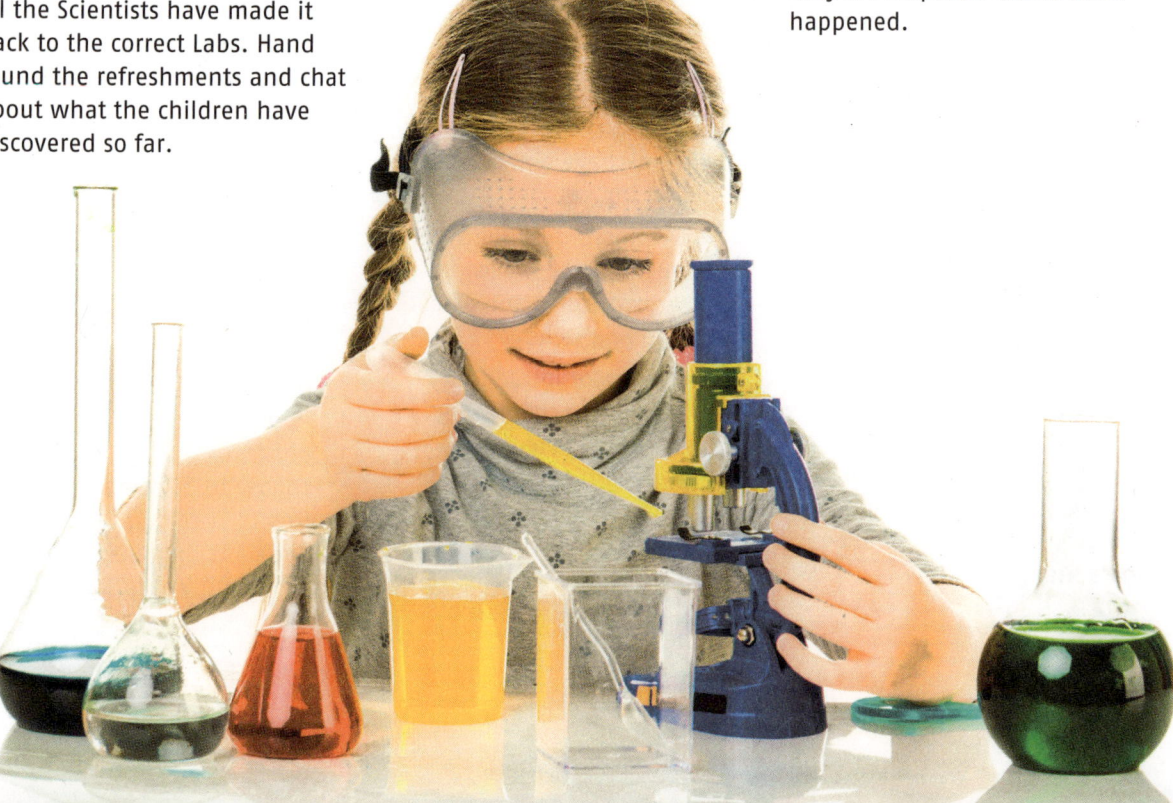

Turn to page 24 and encourage the Scientists to draw pictures from the story. As you do so, chat about why the children chose to draw what they are drawing. What is it that made that bit of the story stand out? This is a way of helping the younger children refine what they thought of the story. Once everyone is finished, compare the pictures and give the Scientists a chance to share what they have drawn, and why.

If you have time, use page 25 to chat about what the children would like to discover next. If any children would like to find out more about God, help them to access their next step, by giving them information about knowing God more or inviting them to the next events you're running.

Time to wonder

Have a time of quiet in your Lab. Ask the group to think about the choice the younger son made when he was looking after the pigs (to go back to his dad and say sorry). Give the children time to consider what they would have done. Then ask the children what they would like to say in response to the story. One of the reasons Jesus told the story was to show that God's love is for everyone, including the Scientists. Would they like to choose to accept God's love and get to know him better?

You might want to have some booklets to help children work through what it might mean for them to decide that they want to follow God. *What Do You Believe?* (for 5 to 8s) and *What is Being a Christian All About?* (for 8 to 11s) are both available from Scripture Union.

Get exploring!

20 minutes in different activities

Hands on

Choose one or more of the experiments on pages 63 to 68 for the Scientists to do. 'Power of instructions' is the most suitable, but select whichever you have the resources and space for. Enjoy discovering new things!

Construction

Show the Scientists your art and craft materials and encourage them to create whatever they like. Alternatively, choose one of the construction ideas from pages 70 to 72; 'Moving figures' is the most suitable, but select whichever you have the resources and space for.

Games

Choose one or more of the games from pages 73 to 76 to play; 'If you love me…' and 'Grand prix' are the most suitable, but select whichever you have the resources and space for.

Scientists' staff room

Ask a few Researchers and Lab Technicians to be in your Time Out area, so that any Scientists who would like to hang out and chat have the chance to do so.

Encourage the children to keep on discovering during this time by providing *The Book of Wonders*, open at pages 104 and 105, and copies of *The Book of Wonders: Activity Book*.

Check your results

20 minutes all together

Call all the Scientists back together and sing the **Wonder Zone** song. Read out any jokes or questions that Scientists have put in the Large Hadron Collider.

A scientist's view

Show the film of a scientist describing how they chose to become Jesus' friend. Alternatively, ask a Researcher or Lab Technician to come to the front and talk about why they chose to be Jesus' friend and what their life was like before and after. (Go through what they are going to say before the session, so that they are confident and happy, and you're sure that it will be suitable for the children in your club).

The appliance of science

Devise another quiz with questions about what has happened at **Wonder Zone** today – include events at the club as well as questions about the Bible story and experiments, and some physical challenges too. Play in Labs or split the Scientists into two teams, playing one side of your space against the other. Make it light-hearted and not too competitive!

Drama: **Discovery Team**

Introduce the drama. Today the Discovery team are sent to the Centre for Clever Robotics to find out about programming and AI.

The knowledge

Before the session, run the *Learn and remember* verse through an online voice synthesiser and record the result.

THE EXPERIMENTS

> '**I praise you because of the wonderful way you created me. Everything you do is marvellous! Of this I have no doubt.**'
> Psalm 139:14 (CEV)

Play the recording and ask the Scientists to join with the electronic voice. Play the recording again, but fade it out for part of the verse. Challenge the Scientists to carry on saying the verse! Do this once more for most and then all of the verse – can people say it without the help of the robotic voice?

Put your heads together

Tell the Scientists that there are lots of different languages that robots and computers use to talk to each other – they may have learned about some of them at school. One language that humans use is sign language. Show the children the BSL (British Sign Language) signs for the words in bold in this prayer (a video is available in the **Wonder Zone** multimedia downloads area). Practise them together and then say this prayer, with everyone joining in with the signs:

I'm **sorry**, **God**, when I have made the wrong **choices**.

Help me to make better **choices**.

Thank you, **God**, for being ready to **welcome** me.

Amen.

Conclusions

Review the day's findings with the Scientists. Chat about the choices we make. Remind the children that we can make a decision to get to know Jesus better, if we want to, and that they can talk about this to their Researchers or Lab Technicians. If there's time, talk about when you made the choice to get to know Jesus better.

Final findings

10 minutes in small groups

Chat with the Scientists about what you explored earlier in your Lab. As the Scientists wait to be collected, they can complete any unfinished pages from their *Lab Books* or *Fact Files*. Alternatively, you could work on any unfinished construction projects or revisit your experiments. Make sure everyone knows about any future events you're running. Say goodbye to each Scientist by name as they leave, making sure they have collected everything they have made during the club.

Decon chamber

It may be that some of the team have their own children at **Wonder Zone** and are unable to stay for long when the programme ends. Try to call everyone together to pray for the Holy Spirit to be at work in the children who have attended **Wonder Zone**. You might like to use this time to discuss together as a team any follow-up activities you are planning.

If you have time and the facilities, the team could share lunch together to round off the club.

LAB EQUIPMENT

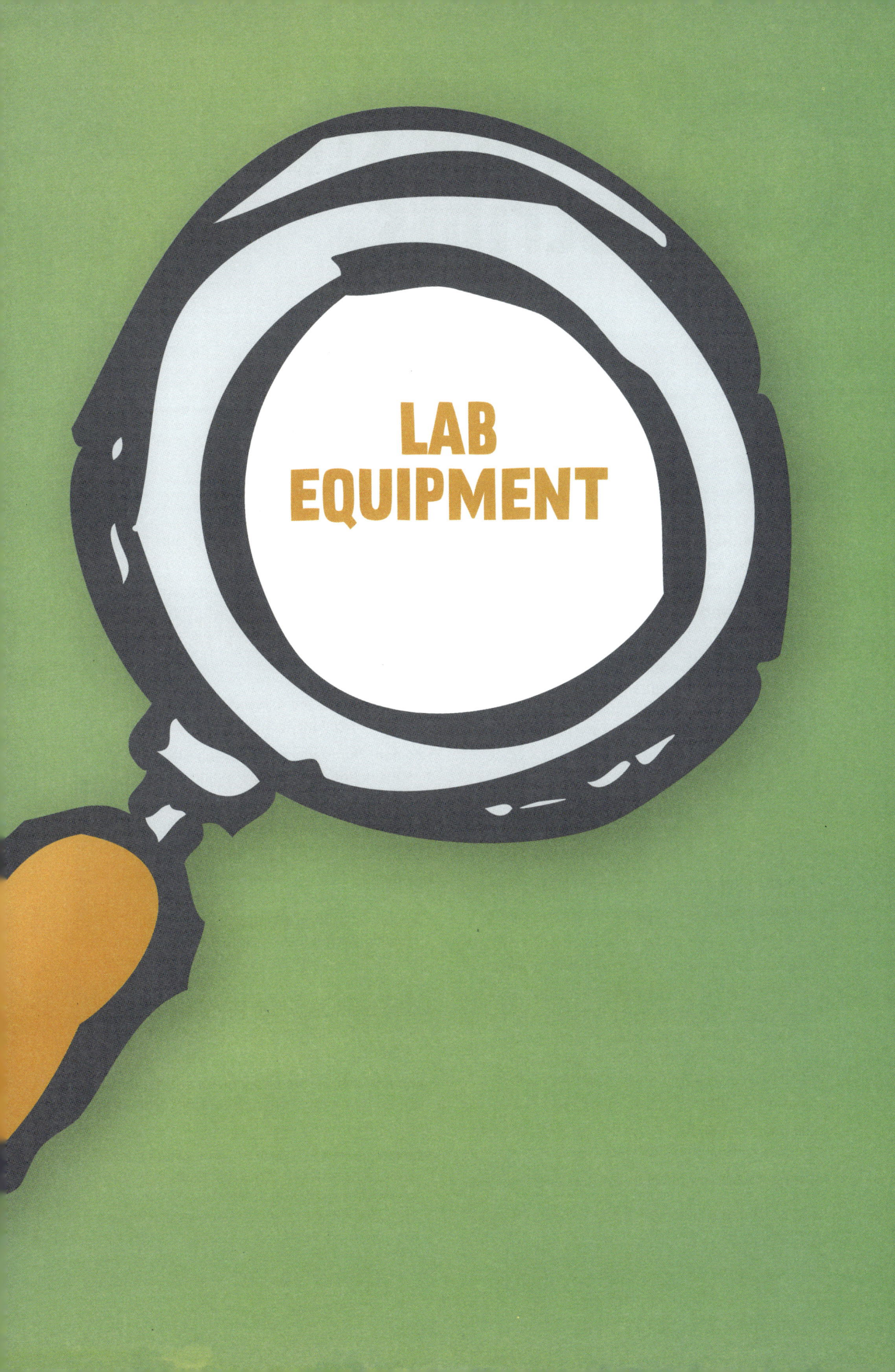

LAB EQUIPMENT

LAB EQUIPMENT 1

Bible story scripts

Experiment 1
King Solomon and the thirst for knowledge

This retelling is performed by one of the Professors and someone playing the part of King Solomon. Encourage them to learn the script and rehearse together before the session.

Professor: Right, everyone, I'm looking for a new Lab Assistant. I've put an advert online and I hope we'll have some good applicants. In fact, the first one should be here any moment.

King Solomon (a leader wearing a crown) enters.

Professor: Ah, here they are now! (*Looks at crown.*) That's an unusual piece of headgear to wear in a laboratory. Why are you wearing a crown?

Solomon: I'm Solomon, King of Israel.

Professor: Israel, eh? I didn't know Israel had a king.

Solomon: Well, not now. I was king about 3,000 years ago.

Professor: What? Have you travelled through time? I wonder if that's possible… I'll have to ask Doctor Who or Professor Brian Cox. Anyway, that's not important now. Have you come to apply for the role of Lab Assistant?

Solomon: Er, no. Not really. I've come to share my story with all the Scientists.

Professor: Are you sure you don't want a new job?

Solomon: No, you're OK. I've got my plate full being king.

Professor: Fair point. I imagine you must be quite busy. So, what's your story?

Solomon: Well, my dad was called David. He was a great king, but when he died, I became king. I wanted to be as good as my dad, so I tried to live the way God wanted me to as much as I could.

Professor: Oh, so you follow God? We're discovering more about following God too!

Solomon: That's why I'm here! You see, I was worshipping God one day when he spoke to me.

Professor: He spoke to you? How did you know it was him?

Solomon: I could hear him! He came to me in a dream. I've been following God all my life. I've always tested whether God was really speaking to me by following his instructions, and it always worked out for good! The more I followed him, the more I got to know his voice.

Professor: Yes, that's a bit like science, building up evidence and understanding over time. What did God say?

Solomon: Well, he made a surprising statement. He said, 'Ask for anything you want, and I will give it to you.'

Professor: Anything?! Ooh, imagine what you could get. A state of the art laboratory, money to pay for research, a super-duper vending machine in the professors' parlour… So what did you ask for?

Solomon: Wisdom. Because to be wise means having knowledge, experience and good judgement about what's right and wrong.

Professor: What? You asked for wisdom? Not even a sports car or speedboat?

Solomon: Nope. I have to rule over a big kingdom, full of lots of people with lots of problems. The most important thing I need is to know things. To know what's right and what's wrong. I need wisdom.

Professor: Wow! You know, that's like me! I like to know things, to discover new ideas and be surprised by the world around me. I also need to know how to decide which things are good to do and which are bad. And did God give you wisdom?

Solomon: Yes! He did! And do you know what? He promised to give me lots of money and a long life too! He really is the best!

Professor: You can get that speedboat after all!

Solomon: Well, no. Sailing is not the most important thing on my to-do list, not when I've got a kingdom to rule.

Professor: So, you don't need a job as a Lab Assistant either, then? I could do with someone with your wisdom.

Solomon: No time, my friend. I'm sure you'll get someone eventually! Bye!

Professor: Bye, your majesty!

LAB EQUIPMENT

Experiment 3
Ben and the power of light

This retelling is performed by one of the Professors and someone playing the part of the blind man (called Ben here). Encourage them to learn the script and rehearse together before the session. As in Experiment 1, the Professor is looking for a new Lab Assistant. If you haven't done Experiment 1, miss out the reference to King Solomon.

Professor: Hello, everyone! I'm still looking for a new Lab Assistant. King Solomon was very wise, but he didn't want the job! I wonder if anyone else will reply to my job advert. (*Looking off-stage.*) Wait a minute. I think someone's coming!

Ben: (*Coming on stage.*) Hello! Great to see you! (*He laughs.*) To see you! I've never said that and actually been able to see the person before! Brilliant! I'm Ben.

Professor: (*Shaking the man's hand.*) Hi, Ben. What do you mean?

Ben: Oh, my goodness, it's a long story. You see – oh! There I go again! You see! (*He laughs again.*) Sorry, I'm still getting my head around what has happened.

Professor: Has something happened? Did you miss the bus on your way to the interview?

Ben: Interview? What interview?

Professor: This interview! For the job of Lab Assistant!

Ben: I'm not here for an interview. I've just met Jesus, and he did something amazing! (*He looks at the children.*) Oh, hello! I didn't see you there... but now I do!

He grabs the Professor and starts to dance. The Professor doesn't really know what's happening.

Professor: Wait! Wait! stop! I feel sick!

Ben: (*Stopping the dancing.*) Oh, sorry. I'm just so happy! Because I was blind, but now I can see! Jesus gave me my sight!

Professor: What? Jesus made you see again?

Ben: Yes! Well, not 'again'. I've never been able to see. But then Jesus came along, spat on the ground, rubbed mud in my eyes and now I can see perfectly.

Professor: What? Jesus put some mud, which was made from his spit, on your eyes? That doesn't sound terribly scientific! It sounds a bit gross to me...

Ben: Well, I didn't really know what was going on. But even if I had known, I wouldn't have said anything: this was Jesus! He's done so many amazing things, I'd trust him completely.

Professor: Your face looks quite clean now though.

Ben: Yes, Jesus told me to wash the mud off in the Pool of Siloam, this large kind of bath in Jerusalem. Siloam actually means 'the one who was sent' – I think Jesus was sent from God to help us!

Professor: Really? Did he say that?

Ben: Kind of. Before he put the mud on my eyes, he said, 'While I am in the world, I am light for the world.'

Professor: What do you think he meant by that?

Ben: Well, he gave me light – everything was dark before he made me see – but I think he meant more than that. When the religious leaders found out what Jesus had done, they made me come and tell them what happened. And I found it funny. I've never been to school; they've been studying the holy books all their lives. But I can see that Jesus is special: he's from God. They can't! They don't know where he's come from! It's like they're the blind people and I'm the one who can see. And, thanks to Jesus, now I can!

Professor: Wow! That's amazing! By the way, you don't want a job as a Lab Assistant, do you?

Ben: I've no time for that. I've met the Son of God and I can't stop telling people about him! It's great to talk about Jesus! Bye, everyone! (*He exits, waving at the children.*)

Professor: Bye! (*To the children.*) Well, that story was mind-blowing. But I've still not got a Lab Assistant...

Experiment 5
Judah and the bad choices

This retelling is performed by one of the Professors and someone playing the part of the younger son (called Judah here). Encourage them to learn the script and rehearse together before the session. As in Experiments 1 and 3, the Professor is looking for a new Lab Assistant. If you haven't done Experiment 1 or 3, miss out the references to the blind man and Solomon.

Professor: Well, my fellow Scientists, I'm still looking for a new Lab Assistant. I've met some interesting people, but none of them wanted the job. Do you remember Ben, the man who was blind but can now see? His story was amazing, but he didn't want to work for me. And what about King Solomon? He was so wise, but didn't have time to work in a laboratory – he had a kingdom to run! I wonder if I'll ever find an assistant...

Judah: (*Entering.*) Hello? Hello?

Professor: Someone's here! They must have come about the job! (*To Judah.*) Hello! Come in, come in! Have you come about the job? Where did you see the advert? In *Science Today*? *The Guardian*? *The Beano*?

Judah: What? Er, no. I don't need a job, thanks, I work with my dad. I did have a job not so long ago, but it wasn't a nice one. I had to look after pigs. Oooh, the smell! My name's Judah, by the way. (*He shakes the Professor's hand.*)

Professor: Pigs? Yes, I suppose they do smell a bit. But they're very intelligent creatures!

Judah: Really? Well, they were probably more intelligent than I was. I'd got myself in a mess and the pig-herding job was when I hit rock bottom.

Professor: What happened? How did you come to be knee-deep in pig manure?

Judah: It's quite embarrassing, actually. I was a bit of an idiot. In fact, I was a massive idiot. You see, I was getting bored at home. All we did was work, work, work. I wanted some excitement! So, I asked my dad for some money.

Professor: How much? £10? £20?

Judah: No. (*He pauses, embarrassed.*) I asked for all the money I would get when my dad died.

Professor: What? Really? What did your dad do?

▶▶

Judah: He was really sad, but he gave me the money anyway. My brother was furious, but I didn't care. I tried to get as far away from my boring family as I could. I ended up in this place where there was so much to do – parties, new friends, new things to try. It was everything my home wasn't.

Professor: If it was so good, why aren't you still there?

Judah: My money ran out. And, when all my money disappeared, so did all my new friends. Turns out they were only after what they could get out of me. I had nothing. I was miles away from home; I had no friends and no money. And that's when I took the job looking after the pigs.

Professor: What did you do next? (*Sniffs.*) You don't smell much like pigs.

Judah: (*Sniffing his clothes.*) No, well, I don't work there any more. I decided to go home again. I thought about how my father's servants are treated better than I was at the pig farm. So I got the idea to go home and ask to work for my dad as a servant.

Professor: What did he say? Wasn't he still angry with you for taking all that money?

Judah: I thought he would be and I had this speech all worked out, saying how stupid I'd been and how I didn't deserve it, but could I work for him. All the way home, I was practising what I would say. I was still quite a way from home when I saw this figure charging up the hill towards me. It took me a moment to work out who it was. Then I realised – it was my dad!

Professor: Oooh, I bet he was rushing to tell you to get lost. That's what I would have done!

Judah: You couldn't be more wrong! He hurtled towards me and, before I'd even got out the first sentence of my speech, he gave me the most massive hug ever! He was crying and then I was crying... I'm starting to well up now, telling you about it! He took me home, gave me a new robe, some shoes and this fancy ring. And then he threw me this massive party!

Professor: Wow! He forgave you then? That's amazing!

Judah: I know! But then my brother came home and he was really angry. He refused to come to the party. My dad went out to him, I could hear them arguing through the window. My dad told my brother: 'My son, your brother, who I thought was dead, is alive. He was lost, but now he's found! Come and celebrate with us!'

Professor: And how does he feel now?

Judah: He's still angry, but I can understand why. Maybe he'll come round. Anyway, I'd better go.

Professor: Wait! Don't you want to be my Lab Assistant? There are no pigs, I promise!

Judah: I can't, I'm back working with my dad again, and it's great! Anyway, good to chat. Got to go: lots of things to do! Bye!

Professor: (*Waving as Judah exits.*) Oh well, maybe I'll never get a Lab Assistant.

Hands on activities

LAB EQUIPMENT 2

Here is a selection of science experiments and activities that you can do in Labs. One or more of these is recommended in each session, but feel free to choose whichever is appropriate to your space, resources and team.

Experiment 1

Film canister rockets

What you need

- camera film canisters (available online)
- antacid or vitamin tablets (fizzing ones, such as Alka Seltzer)
- water
- safety goggles
- outside space

What you do

1 Give each Scientist a film canister. Show them how to take the top off the canister and put one teaspoon of water in the bottom.

2 Give everyone half an antacid tablet. In turn, wearing a pair of safety goggles, invite each Scientist to drop the half tablet in the canister and snap the lid on very quickly. Turn the canister upside-down (so that the lid is on the floor) and retreat to a safe distance. After around ten seconds, the canister will fly into the air with a pop! (If the rocket doesn't pop, wait about 30 seconds before going back to it.)

3 You could add extra bits on to your canisters (such as fins made of card or extra decoration) to see if it improves the flight of the rocket! (But make sure you still place the lid on quickly!)

The science bit: when the water touches the antacid tablet, it starts to dissolve it, giving off carbon dioxide. The carbon dioxide gas builds up in the canister until the pressure is so great that it blasts the canister into the air! If the rocket doesn't work, the cap probably wasn't on properly, allowing the gas to escape.

Litmus test

What you need

- pH test paper (available cheaply online)
- around ten different liquids to test
- yogurt pots
- pens
- paper

What you do

1 Before the session, gather together some different common liquids to test with the paper, eg milk, water, brown sauce, passata or tomato juice, puréed broccoli, lemon juice, washing-up liquid. Put them in the (clean) yogurt pots and label them 1 to 10.

2 Invite the Scientists to form pairs, and give each pair some pH test paper, a litmus colour chart, a sheet of paper and a pen. Encourage them to draw a two-column table on the sheet of paper and write 'Number of pot' at the top of one column and 'pH number' at the top of the other.

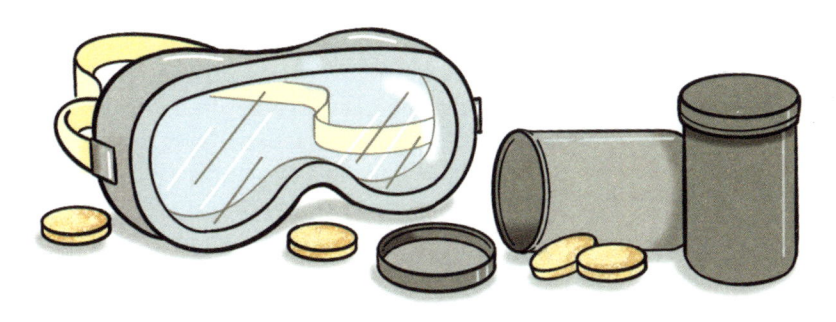

LAB EQUIPMENT

3 Show them how to dip the pH test paper into the liquid and watch it change colour (they might have to wipe the excess liquid off to see the colour properly!). Encourage them to compare the test-paper colour to their chart to see what the pH number is. Below 7 and the liquid is acidic; above 7 and it's an alkali. Once everyone has finished, compare your findings.

The science bit: the paper reacts with the liquid in different ways, depending on whether it's an acid or alkali. Acids include things like lemon juice or the liquid in car batteries. Acidic food can cause our teeth to erode, if we don't neutralise it (by drinking some milk or chewing gum, for example).

Experiment 2

DIY solar system

What you need

- a map of the solar system
- nine balls or balloons of different sizes
- access to the internet
- a large outside space
- a tape measure
- chalk

What you do

1 Gather the Scientists around the map of the solar system and make sure everyone is familiar with all the planets (you could refer back to pages 12 and 13 of *Lab Book*.) Put your balls and/or balloons in size order, then assign the balls/balloons the names of planets from smallest to largest: Mercury, Mars, Venus, Earth, Neptune, Uranus, Saturn and Jupiter. Finally, call the largest ball/balloon the Sun. Go on the internet to find out how quickly each planet goes around the Sun (make sure you supervise internet access).

2 Ask each Scientist to choose a planet or Sun. Put the Sun in the middle of your outside space and draw eight concentric circles around the Sun on the floor with the chalk. Station the other planets in the order of their orbits, and then ask the Scientists to orbit the sun according to how quickly their planet goes. They should all go anticlockwise.

3 For a few seconds, encourage the Scientists to turn around as they orbit, to represent the spin of the planets. The Sun and all the planets except Venus and Uranus should go anticlockwise. Venus and Uranus should go clockwise. (Don't do this for long, as the Scientists will get dizzy and may fall over!)

4 You could also explore the comparative distances the planets are from the Sun. Find a chart of distances online and use a scale of 1 AU to 1 m. AU stands for Astronomical Unit and is the distance the Earth is from the Sun. Your Earth would be 1 m from your Sun; Neptune would be 30 m away!

The science bit: the solar system was formed when a giant molecular cloud collapsed. As it collapsed the cloud started to rotate faster and faster, flattening into a disc, with everything spinning around a proto-star. Gravity gathered dust and gas together into larger objects – the planets. There may have been lots of planets, but they got destroyed or merged together into larger bodies.

Clay planets

What you need
- air-drying clay
- water
- a picture of the Moon
- small pebbles
- cover-up and clean-up equipment

What you do

1 Make sure everyone is well covered up and that you have covered your work surfaces with newspaper or wipe-clean tablecloths.

2 Give each Scientist a lump of clay and ask them to shape it into a smooth ball. They may need to use a little water to make the clay easier to smooth down. Think about the planets and moons, including the Earth and Moon. Are they smooth like your clay spheres? Compare your clay planets with the picture of the Moon.

3 Ask the Scientists to imagine what might make planets and moons pockmarked. There are lots of small objects flying around our solar system – asteroids and meteoroids. When they hit a planet or moon, they leave a mark! Give out the pebbles and encourage the Scientists to crash them into their smooth planet. They should see their clay sphere become covered in craters.

The science bit: most meteoroids and asteroids in our neighbourhood of space were left over from the creation of the solar system. When meteoroids or asteroids land on a planet or moon, they are called meteorites. The Moon has barely any atmosphere and so is left open to bits of space rock hitting it. The Earth is protected by its atmosphere and most objects burn up or fragment in the atmosphere (these are what shooting stars are), or sometimes are deflected off the edge of the atmosphere.

Experiment 3

Cress head

What you need
- clean half egg shells
- eggboxes cut into sections
- cotton wool
- water
- cress seeds
- felt-tip pens
- large yogurt pots (or similar)
- black paper
- sticky tape

What you do

1 Give each Scientist two half egg shells and two sections of eggbox. Encourage them to decorate their egg shells with faces (perhaps one happy and one sad) and then to put each one in a section of eggbox.

2 Help the Scientists to half fill each shell with cotton wool and dampen with water, then sow some cress seeds on to the cotton wool.

3 Give each Scientist a yogurt pot and ask them to wrap it in black paper, so very little light can get through it.

4 You can do this experiment at your venue or invite the Scientists to take their cress heads home to do the experiment. Place both egg shells on a sunny windowsill and place the yogurt pot upside-down over one of them. Make sure both shells are well watered but keep one of them covered up. Watch to see what happens with how the cress grows. The one in the sunlight should grow normally, with little green leaves. The covered one won't be green and will grow more 'stringy'!

The science bit: most plants need light to grow healthily, turning sunlight and carbon dioxide into food. Plants deprived of light will still grow, but will put all their energy into sending up shoots to reach light as soon as possible, meaning they grow tall and thin.

Diffraction goggles

What you need
- copies of the spectacles template from page 91
- scissors
- felt-tip pens
- sticky tape
- diffraction grating sheets (available online in rolls)
- paper and pens

What you do
1 Copy the spectacles template on to thin card and help the children to cut out their spectacles, including the space for the lenses. Encourage them to colour in the frames however they want. As they work, chat about what you have discovered today. Ask if anyone wears glasses – what is it like? If you wear glasses, show them yours!

2 Cut out pieces of the diffraction grating sheets just large enough to cover the lens holes of the glasses and stick them on to the frame. Put the glasses on and challenge the children to describe to each other what they can see. Warn them not to look directly at bright lights, and particularly not the sun.

3 Encourage the children to write or draw what they can see and how it changes as they move their eyes or head around.

The science bit: the diffraction grating sheets have ridges, called rulings, that split or diffract the light. The light hits the ridges at different angles and so we see different colours of the spectrum in different patterns.

Experiment 4

Experiments about me

What you need
- a 2-litre plastic bottle
- a length of rubber tubing
- a large tub of water
- a marker pen
- a measuring jug
- ink pads
- paper and pens
- magnifying glasses
- cover-up and clean-up equipment

What you do
These experiments tell us something about our bodies and brains!

1 For the first experiment, place the bottle in the water and let it fill up. Lift it upside-down part of the way out of the water, making sure that the mouth of the bottle is still submerged. Place one end of the tubing into the water and up into the mouth of the bottle. Invite a Scientist to take a deep breath and blow into the other end of the tubing. They should keep going until they have no breath left. Keeping a thumb over the end of the tube, mark the line of the water on the bottle. Refill the bottle, wash the end of the tubing and invite the other Scientists to have a go. The amount of water displaced is equal to the capacity of our lungs. To find out the capacity, take the bottle out of the water, fill it up to one of the lines and then pour the water into a measuring jug.

2 For the second experiment, invite the Scientists to make a circle with the thumb and forefinger of one hand. Choose an object across the room and, with the circle at arm's length, challenge them to look at the object through the circle, trying to get it in middle. Now ask them to close one eye and then the other. Say that if they close an eye and the object seems to jump out of the circle, they have just closed their dominant eye!

The science bit: our brains form pictures of the world around us using the information it gets through our eyes. It will favour one eye over the other, meaning when it has a choice, such as the one you gave it when you looked through the circle, it will always choose one eye over the other.

3 For the third experiment you could explore fingerprints. Invite the Scientists to draw five squares on a sheet of paper. Show them how to roll the ends of each of their fingers and the thumb of one hand on the ink pad and print out a fingerprint in each box, labelling which one is which. Encourage them to look at the prints through a magnifying glass and try to pick out patterns and repeated features. If you have access to the internet, search for common patterns in fingerprints (or print them out before the session). What patterns can they spot in their own fingerprints? Are any the same? (Make sure the fingerprints are either taken home or destroyed at the end of the session.)

Insect castle

What you need

- clay plant pots
- bamboo canes
- scissors
- string
- wax (and the means to melt it)

What you do

1 Before the club, cut the bamboo canes into the right length to sit neatly in the plant pots (there may be someone in your congregation who can do this for you).

2 Give each Scientist a plant pot and some lengths of bamboo canes and show them how to tie the canes into small bundles with the string (this makes them easier to handle).

3 Melt some wax in a microwave and pour some into the bottom of each pot (being careful not to let it dribble out of the holes in the bottom). Help the Scientists to stick the ends of their bundles of cane into the wax, securing the canes into the pot. (You could also use play dough or similar to fix the canes in the pot.)

4 Invite the Scientists to take their pot home and place it in a damp shady spot in their garden. If children don't have any outside space, you could arrange to place them in your church grounds. Encourage them to go back in a couple of days', a week's and a month's time to see what kinds of insects they can see going in and out of the insect castle!

The science bit: many insects thrive in cool, dark, damp places and creating this castle will give them somewhere to live. It also gives children the chance to observe the insects and count the different kinds without trapping or killing them.

Experiment 5

Technical toys

What you need

- technical construction toys, such as Lego Technic or Meccano (you might have someone in your congregation or community who can lend these to you)

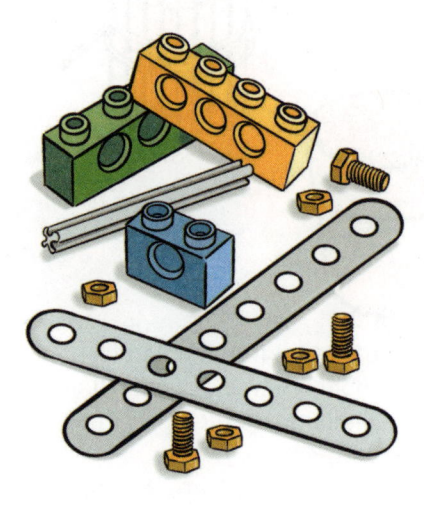

What you do

1 Show the Scientists the different technical toys you have collected. Encourage them to explore and create whatever they want. You might have some manuals to help create specific toys or machines. Have these on hand to help those Scientists who are struggling to create something. Have plenty of team on hand to help (though don't be tempted to take over – let the Scientists take the lead!).

2 Once you have finished, invite the Scientists to demonstrate what they have created.

The science bit: the Scientists will have used motors, levers and more to create their model. Talk through what each part does – for example, turning electrical energy into kinetic energy to move wheels or cogs.

Power of instructions

What you need

- blindfolds
- balls
- baskets or buckets
- chalk or masking tape

What you do

1 Before the session, mark out several paths from one side to the other. Make the turns at right angles to make them easier to follow. Place a basket or bucket at the end of each path.

2 Ask the group to think about instructions and commands that are given to robots. How accurate do those need to be?

3 Put the Scientists into pairs. Blindfold one of the children in each pair and give the blindfolded child a ball.

4 Challenge the sighted Scientist to give their partner a set of instructions to guide them around one of the paths and drop the ball into their basket. But they have to give all the instructions before their partner sets out.

5 Once they have finished, swap roles and move to a different path.

6 After the first run, chat about how easy or difficult it was to give commands. How easy was it to remember and follow those commands?

7 Go for a second run, but this time without the blindfolds. Observe how the pairs communicate. Does the partner on the path give advice to or ask for clarification from the guide?

8 After both in the pairs have had a go without a blindfold, chat about how they reacted when they were being guided, but could see. How differently does AI respond to instructions? Many now will learn and adapt the way they achieve their objectives.

Art and construction

LAB EQUIPMENT 3

Free-choice

Although it is nice to have a craft project that the children can aim towards, it might be more beneficial to let the children create whatever they like in response to the story they have explored. This has two benefits:

1 It fosters children's creativity – they will often come up with ingenious and creative ideas when given free rein with a set of resources. Also, this freedom is not something they are often given. Much of their time – at school, at home and at church – is directed towards specific aims.

2 It fosters children's spirituality – it might well be that God has been saying different things to different children in your Lab through the same story. To have a prescribed construction end point might well squash the conversation that the child is having with God; what a child has been reflecting on may not be the same as the aim of the prescribed craft. Giving children the freedom to explore faith through craft means that it becomes an extension of Bible exploration, and gives children time to continue their conversation with Jesus naturally and more deeply.

Practically, here are some suggestions of what you might provide. You don't have to have all of these, just choose the ones that you have or can borrow:

- Art materials: paint and paintbrushes, white paper, coloured paper, felt-tip pens, crayons, pencil crayons, pencils
- Craft materials: stickers, craft foam, sequins, glitter, felt, tissue paper, card, wallpaper off-cuts, lolly sticks, craft straws, scissors, glue sticks
- Construction toys: wooden blocks (eg building blocks or a Jenga game), plastic blocks (such as Lego or Duplo), Meccano
- Natural tactile materials: sandpaper, sand, pebbles, sticks, smooth wooden objects (such as holding crosses or wooden eggs), teasels, dried flowers
- Books: children's Bible storybooks, children's Bibles, the *Book of Wonders*, atlases, picture books, Bible information books, notebooks and pens for journalling
- Clean-up and cover-up equipment: dustpan and brush, dusters, aprons and overalls, soapy water and towels, newspaper, wipe-clean mats and tablecloths.

Set out everything you have gathered on tables around the edge of the space, and invite the Scientists, in small groups of three or four, to go and choose what they would like to work with. Make sure you have Researchers and/or Lab Technicians on hand to help children access the materials. Make sure Scientists know that they can share, so it's OK if someone chooses what they want to use.

As the children work, circulate around the space, chatting with the Scientists about the club and that session's story. Let the Scientists guide the conversation, asking questions to help them clarify what they have discovered about God and their relationship with him. At the end of your construction time, reassure the children that they can finish their projects at home or the next time you meet.

LAB EQUIPMENT

Junk modelling

Before the club, collect together lots of junk items, such as boxes, eggboxes, cardboard tubes, foil, scraps of fabric, yogurt pots – indeed, anything clean from your recycling bin! You will also need sticky tape, glue sticks, scissors, coloured paper, felt-tip pens and other art materials. For each experiment, challenge the Scientists to create a different model from the junk provided!

- **Experiment 1**: an erupting volcano (mirroring the exploding experiments they have done) or something general about science
- **Experiment 2**: a rocket or space station
- **Experiment 3**: something that gives off light, such as a lighthouse
- **Experiment 4**: an animal
- **Experiment 5**: a robot

You could choose to have one project that runs over all the sessions of **Wonder Zone**. Challenge the Scientists to create an ingenious machine that achieves a specific aim, such as moving an egg from one point to another.

Activities based on daily themes

Experiment 1

Splash paintings

What you need
- large sheets of paper
- poster paint in different colours
- unused toothbrushes
- pipettes (optional)
- cover-up and clean-up equipment

What you do
1. Cover your table or space with newspaper (or do this activity outside).
2. Give out the paper and show the different colours of paint. Explain to the children how to dip the toothbrushes into paint and flick it so that it sprays on to the paper. Explore how it looks like a fountain or explosion.
3. Encourage the children to experiment with different colours to create different patterns. If you have pipettes, help them to squeeze paint into the pipette and then squirt it on the paper to create a different fountain pattern.
4. As you work, chat about what the children have explored so far, including the exploding experiment in Lab practice.

70

3 • ART AND CONSTRUCTION

Experiment 2
Space and stars

What you need
- large sheets of paper
- crayons or candles
- black or dark blue poster paint
- paintbrushes
- cover-up and clean-up equipment

What you do

1 Give out the sheets of paper and encourage the children to draw a starscape using the crayons or candles. They could draw anything they might see in space, such as planets, stars, comets, spaceships or satellites!

2 Once they have finished, show them how to paint over their picture with the black or dark blue paint. The crayon or candle pictures should repel the paint and so show through to create a beautiful night sky! (Try this out beforehand to make sure the effect works with the crayons or candles you are using.)

3 As you work, chat about what the children know about space, and what they have discovered already at **Wonder Zone**. Encourage an air of wonder and awe about the scale and beauty of the universe, reminding them of the words of Psalm 8.

Experiment 3
Rainbow

What you need
- large sheets of paper
- collage materials
- art materials
- PVA glue or glue sticks
- scissors
- cover-up and clean-up equipment

What you do

1 You could work as individuals on this, or create a piece of artwork as a group – let the children decide how they want to work.

2 Draw a large rainbow on the paper and then either colour or paint the stripes in the correct colours, or stick on collage materials to fill them in. Encourage the group to be creative about their collage choices – they could use wool, ribbons or photos from magazines as well as coloured paper.

3 As you work, chat about what you have discovered about light today, as well as the Bible story. What do they think Jesus meant when he said he was 'light for the world'?

71

LAB EQUIPMENT

Experiment 4
Animal printing

What you need

- large sheets of paper
- poster paint
- sponges
- paintbrushes
- pictures of animals with different patterned skin, fur or feathers
- cover-up and clean-up equipment

What you do

1 Show the children the animal pictures you have brought and chat about the different colours and patterns they have on their skin, fur or feathers.

2 Invite the group to recreate some of those colours or patterns with poster paint. They could paint or print the different patterns.

3 Alternatively, challenge the children to come up with their own animal patterns and prints. How creative can they be?

4 As you work, talk about the great diversity of plants and animals on Earth. Talk about people and how diverse and amazing they are, too!

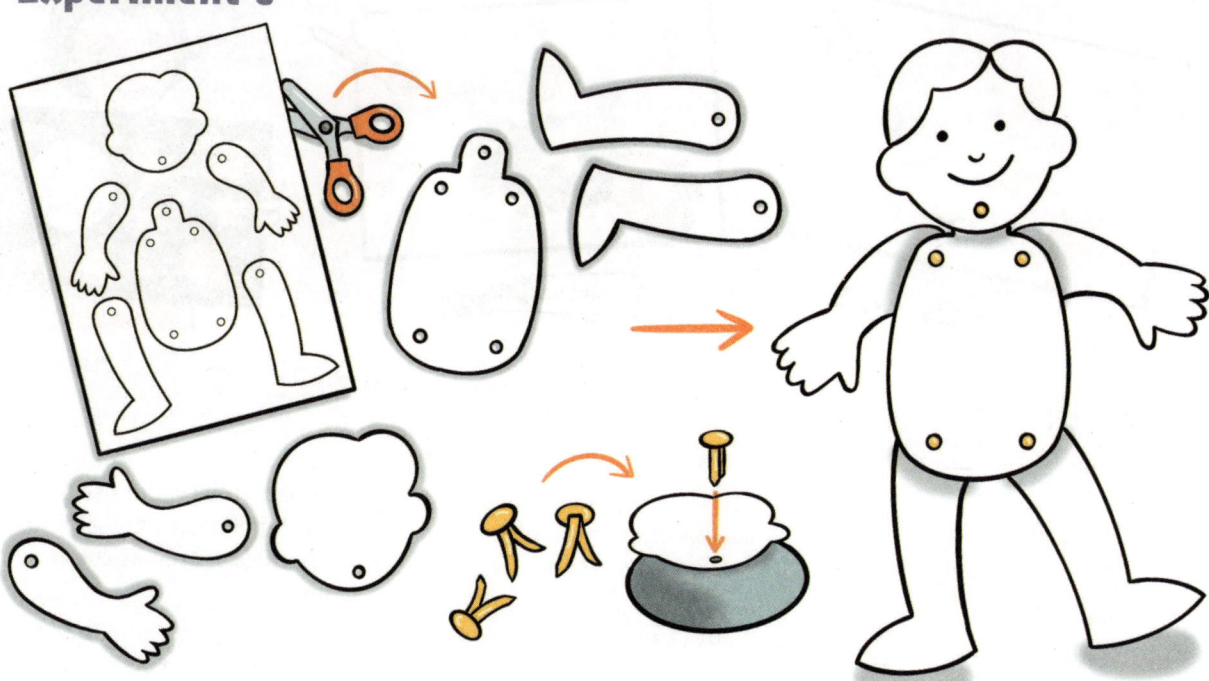

Experiment 5
Moving figures

What you need

- body-part templates (from page 92)
- pencils
- card
- scissors
- felt-tip pens
- split pins
- sticky tack or play dough

What you do

1 Give out the templates and encourage the children to draw round all the pieces on to card. Help them to cut these out and then decorate them using the felt-tip pens. Give everyone a blob of sticky tack or play dough and show them how to join all the pieces together using the split pins (push the pin through the pieces into the sticky tack or playdough to avoid the children hurting their fingers).

2 Have fun moving your figures and putting them in different positions. As you do so, chat about what the children have discovered today about robots, and also about the Bible story.

72

Games activities

LAB EQUIPMENT 4

Choose a selection of these games for your session. You might wish to keep the theme of each Experiment, or just play the ones your Scientists will enjoy!

Experiment 1

Exploding canisters

What you need
- a film canister (or a soft ball)
- music

What you do

1 Invite the players to stand in a circle, and give one player the film canister. As you play the music, the players must throw the canister to each other.

2 At a random point, stop the music. The person holding the canister when the music stops is out! You can pretend that the film canister rocket has exploded at this point, and encourage the player to mime exploding with the canister! You might have to watch for a bit of cheating when the music stops…

3 The last two players left are the winners. You might also want to award points or prizes to the best 'exploders'! (For younger children, it might be easier to use a soft ball, rather than a canister.)

Fact finding

What you need
- copies of 'Wonderous facts' from the **Wonder Zone** multimedia downloads area

What you do

1 Give the Scientists each a copy of 'Wonderous facts', and challenge them to find their three favourite facts from the list. Help children who are reluctant readers to access the material.

2 Ask the Scientists to list their three best discoveries. Invite everyone to read out their facts and vote for the best ones. Did anyone choose the same facts?

LAB EQUIPMENT

Experiment 2
Solar system target bowls

What you need
- tennis-ball-size balls
- a large sheet of paper
- marker pens
- chalk or masking tape

What you do

1. Before the session, draw out a target with the Sun at the centre and the orbits of Venus, Mars, Saturn and Neptune. The outer circle (the orbit of Neptune) should be around 1.5 m in diameter. Place the target at one end of your space, then mark a line about 5 m away from the target.

2. Challenge the Scientists to stand behind the line and roll a ball towards the target. The aim is to get as close to the Sun as possible. You could play individually, or in teams (with sets of balls of the same colour so you know which ball belongs to which team). Award points or prizes to those who get closest to the Sun!

Black hole

What you need
- chalk or masking tape
- music

What you do

1. Draw some galaxy shapes on the floor with chalk (or mark them out with masking tape), making them large enough for four or five children to stand in at the same time. Give the shapes galactic names, such as Andromeda, Milky Way, Centaurus A, Whirlpool and Sombrero, and write these next to the galaxies. (Make sure you get roughly the right shapes for the galaxies you're drawing. Check online for examples.)

2. Play some music and encourage the Scientists to dance around. When you stop the music, the Scientists should choose a galaxy to stand in. With your back to the playing area, call out the name of a galaxy. This galaxy gets swallowed up by a black hole and the Scientists in it are out! Keep playing until you have a winner. (You could play non-competitively, where those swallowed by a black hole sit out the next round, but then start playing again.)

3. You could also play some of the games on the NASA website: spaceplace.nasa.gov/menu/play/

Experiment 3
Blindfold search

What you need
- a ball pit filled with balls
- blindfolds
- various objects to find
- a stopwatch

What you do

1. Before the session, collect together a range of different objects such as a torch, some sunglasses, a toy car or a toy camera. Mix these into the ball pit.

2. Invite the Scientists to form pairs, and blindfold one of the pair. Guide the blindfolded player into the ball pit. Shout out the name of the objects in the ball pit. The sighted player has to guide their partner to where that is, so that they can pick it up and remove it from the pit. Keep going until all the items have been found. Time each pair to see who can finish in the shortest time.

3. Alternatively, have two ball pits with the same objects, and play one pair against another.

4 • GAMES ACTIVITIES

Experiment 4

Candle, tornado, room

What you do

1 This game is like rock, paper, scissors, but with bigger actions!

2 Invite the Scientists to form pairs. On the count of three, encourage each player to choose either candle, tornado or room (and do the action!). Candle lights room, room keeps out tornado, tornado blows out candle. If they each choose the same thing, they should play again until there's a winner. The winner of each pair then finds another winner and plays them. At the end, you should be left with one winner!

- **Candle**: the player should wave their hands like a flame and say 'Candle' in a high voice.
- **Tornado**: the player should spin around and shout 'Tornado!' as loudly as they can.
- **Room**: the player should stand with their arms and legs out wide and shout 'Roooooooooooooom' in a deep voice.

3 Challenge the Scientists to come up with other light-based versions of the game.

The king of the jungle

What you need

- chairs

What you do

1 Invite the Scientists to sit in a circle. Ask everyone to choose an animal and think up an action and sound effect they can do to represent their animal. A leader should be the lion and come up with an appropriate leonine action.

2 In turn, ask each player to demonstrate their action and sound in order from the lion's left, clockwise around the circle until you get to the player on the lion's right, who is at the bottom. Once everyone knows the animals and actions, the lion, as the king of the jungle, starts the game.

3 The lion performs their own action and sound, followed by that of another animal. Encourage this animal to do their own action and sound, followed by another.

4 The game continues until a player gets an action or sound wrong, misses their own action or hesitates too long. This player goes to the bottom of the order and everyone shifts up one. Players do not keep their own animal but take over the animal of the previous player to sit in that seat! The idea is to dislodge the player sitting in the king of the jungle's seat!

Animal obstacles

What you need

- equipment for a simple obstacle course
- a stopwatch (optional)

What you do

1 Before the session, set up a simple obstacle course and risk assess it so that children don't get hurt. In your course, leave some sections free of obstacles, so that children can do impressions of how different animals move.

2 Play this game in Labs and time the runs, or split Labs in half to play against each other. Show the Scientists your course and, in the sections free of obstacles, tell the children what animals they need to imitate. For example, they could hop like a kangaroo, slither like a snake, mime flying like a bird or walk on four legs like a cat.

3 Alternatively, you could theme each obstacle and challenge the children to behave like a certain animal on each one. For example, they could 'balance like a lemur' along a log (line marked on the floor), 'hop the lily pads (rugs laid out on floor) like a frog' or 'suck like an anteater' (moving marshmallows from one bowl to another with a straw).

4 You could award points or prizes for the fastest Labs, and also for the best kangaroo/snake/bird impressions!

75

LAB EQUIPMENT

Experiment 5

If you love me...

What you do

1 Invite all the players to sit in a circle (on the floor or on chairs), with one player in the middle.

2 Challenge the player in the middle to go up to someone in the circle and say, 'Honey, if you love me, you'll smile.' The player in the circle must say, 'Honey, I love you, but I just can't smile.' And they must say this without smiling. If they manage to avoid smiling, the player in the middle moves on to someone else and says the same thing. If they smile, then they take over as the player in the middle.

3 The player in the middle can experiment with different ways of saying their line to make it as funny as possible!

Grand prix

What you need
- remote-control cars
- chalk or masking tape
- small obstacles

What you do

1 Before the session, mark out a course with chalk or masking tape and place some small obstacles around the course to create ramps, chicanes or road blocks.

2 Place the remote-control cars at the start and invite the Scientists to choose which car they want to control.

3 On the word 'Go!', challenge the players to race around the course to try and be the first over the finish line. If your course is short, you could race for three or five laps. You might need to have a few marshals around the course to rescue any cars that crash or to keep an eye out for any cheating!

Drama scripts

LAB EQUIPMENT 5

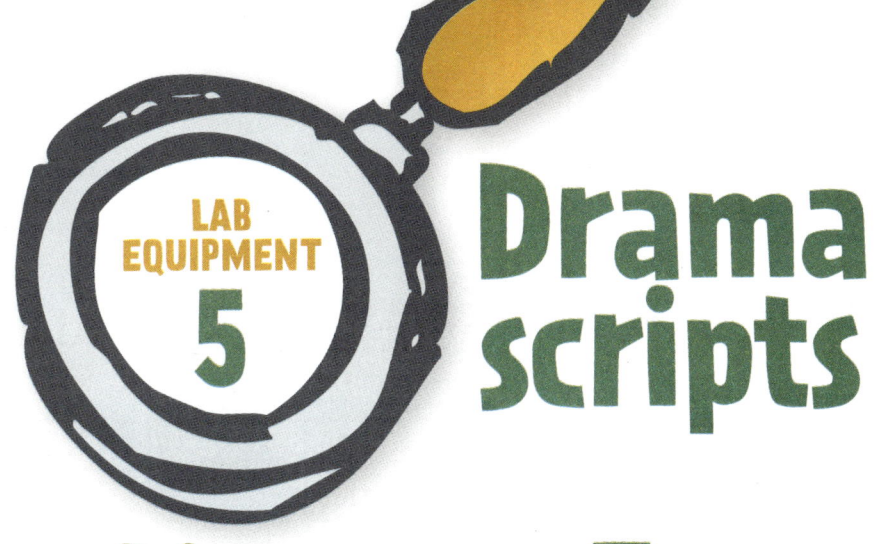

Discovery Team

The **Wonder Zone** is a centre of research and discovery. At its disposal, it has technology and equipment beyond the wildest dreams of most scientists. In each Experiment, Rosalind, the head of scientific discovery at the **Wonder Zone**, sends the Discovery team off in their futuristic transporter to investigate scientific phenomena.

For each Experiment, you'll need the transporter on one side of the stage. This could be as simple as some chairs (two in front, two behind, like a car) or as elaborate as the set of *Star Wars*!

The drama will work best if the team are able to learn the script and have time to rehearse, so that the slapstick sections are well-choreographed and run smoothly.

Cast

- **Rosalind** – the head of scientific discovery at Wonder Zone
- **Blessing** – a top scientist
- **Brandon** – her research assistant
- **Yasmin** – the lab assistant and mechanic
- **Kyle** – the cleaner
- **Some ants** (non-speaking) (Experiment 4 only)
- **Voice of the public address system/robot control** (Experiment 5 only)
- **Director of the Centre of Clever Robotics** (Experiment 5 only)
- **Assistant at the Centre of Clever Robotics** (Experiment 5 only)
- **Other assistants** (non-speaking)

The characters can be played as any gender or ethnic background. Simply change the names to suit the actors taking part.

You will only need basic costumes. Rosalind and the Director of the Centre of Clever Robotics should wear business clothes; the scientists and assistants will need lab coats; Kyle should have a tabard. The ants can dress in black with simple masks; extra legs can be created using stuffed black tights.

LAB EQUIPMENT

Experiment 1
The fun of discovery

Rosalind walks on stage, talking into her mobile phone.

Rosalind: Yes, Prime Minister. I'm sure the appearance of giant locusts in Number 10 was a one-off. And I'm sure the Downing Street cat will recover in a few days. If it happens again, I'll send the Discovery team to investigate. Bye. Yes, of course. Bye.

She taps on the phone to finish the call, then looks up. She notices the children.

Rosalind: Ah! The Scientists are here! Good to have you with us! I'm Professor Rosalind Goodall, head of scientific discovery at the **Wonder Zone**. Here, we investigate the biggest, best and most intriguing scientific phenomena! (*She checks her watch.*) Excellent! You'll soon be able to meet the Discovery team; they're due here any minute now.

She looks off to stage left. From stage right, we hear the noise of vacuuming as Kyle comes on stage, pushing a vacuum cleaner. He has headphones in and is singing a pop song the children will know.

Rosalind: (*Shouting over the noise of the vacuum cleaner.*) **Kyle! Kyle! What are you doing?** (*He doesn't hear her.*) **Kyle!** (*She walks over to him, but he turns his back on her and vacuums in the other direction.*) **Kyle!**

She taps him on the shoulder and he screams.

Kyle: (*Recovering, turning off the vacuum cleaner and taking his headphones off.*) Oh, Prof! You frightened me to death! How's it going? Made any more amazing discoveries yet?

Rosalind: What are you doing the cleaning for? I've got all these Scientists here ready to do some top-level research. They can't concentrate if you're spraying and polishing all the day long.

Kyle: Sorry, Prof, I thought you and the team were out today.

Rosalind: They're on their way. We've had some interesting readings from a volcano in Iceland and I need to send them off to investigate.

There are noises off stage and the team hurry on stage left, led by Blessing. Brandon follows, eating a large sandwich. Yasmin brings up the rear, carrying lots of bags and suitcases.

Blessing: Brandon, what is in that sandwich? It smells disgusting!

Brandon: It's sausage, piccalilli, lemon curd, coleslaw, jam, ham, spam and lamb. (*He offers it to Blessing.*) Fancy a bite?

Blessing: No! (*She sees Rosalind.*) Hello, Prof. We're ready to go. What's the mission this time?

Rosalind: You're off to Iceland. There's a volcano there that's giving off some very interesting readings. I need you to investigate. The transporter is all ready to go.

Blessing: Great! Yasmin, get all that equipment on to the transporter.

Yasmin totters towards the transporter with all the baggage. She gets halfway and then drops everything.

Kyle: (*Going over to Yasmin.*) Here, let me give you a hand.

Yasmin: Thanks, Kyle.

Kyle: (*Struggling to pick up a bag.*) Wow! What's in this? It weighs a tonne!

Yasmin: That one? That's Brandon's sandwich suitcase. He never goes anywhere without 15 tins of luncheon meat.

Kyle: Eurgh.

Yasmin and Kyle load the bags into the transporter. As they do so, Kyle gets trapped in the transporter by the luggage and can't get out. While this is happening, Rosalind talks to Blessing.

Rosalind: (*Showing a smartphone to Blessing.*) I've got all these readings. You need to look at them before you get to the volcano. (*She taps the screen.*) Right, if you look at these figures here...

Blessing: No time for that now. We'll check them out on the flight there. (*Looking over at Yasmin.*) Right, have we got everything? Let's go!

Kyle: (*Muffled.*) Help!

Rosalind: Did you say something, Blessing?

Blessing: No.

78

Kyle: (*Muffled.*) Help!

Rosalind: There it is again.

Yasmin: Oh, hang on. I know what that is: it's Brandon's stomach. It always does that after he's had one of his super-sub sandwiches. It's grim.

Brandon: Hey! My stomach is just appreciating the best sandwich-making in the business! Come on, we'd better get going if we're going to get to Iceland before dinner time.

They all pile into the transporter.

Rosalind: Safe travels, everyone! I've sent the readings from the volcano to your smartphones. Check them out before you land. (*She exits.*)

Kyle: (*Muffled.*) Help!

Blessing: Brandon, keep your stomach under control!

She starts the transporter. There is a sound effect of an engine. Blessing, Brandon and Yasmin pretend to take off, then lean from side to side as if they were turning left and right. Kyle can be heard shouting for help every so often.

Yasmin: Blessing, shouldn't we look at those readings now? Prof said they were important.

Blessing: No need. We'll be there in a minute. And nothing beats live readings and observation!

After a minute, Blessing lands the transporter.

Blessing: Right, here we are – Iceland! Let's get out and see what's going on.

Blessing, Yasmin and Brandon get out of the transporter and walk across the stage, treading carefully as they go. They carry scientific-looking equipment and tablets to take readings from the volcano.

Brandon: Is it hot or is it me?

Yasmin: What's that smell? It's like rotten eggs! (*She pinches her nose.*)

Blessing: That's the sulphur. You often get that with geothermal activity.

They gather in a group at the front of the stage on the opposite side to the transporter, examining their smartphones, taking readings. Kyle pushes some of the luggage out of his way and emerges from where he's been trapped.

Kyle: Phew! I thought I'd never get out. Where am I? On a volcano? Oh no! (*He notices something on the floor of the transporter.*) What's this? (*He picks up a smartphone and taps the screen.*) Wait a minute, these readings say that the volcano will erupt any minute! We've got to get out of here!

Kyle leaps into the driver's seat and 'starts' the transporter. Everyone on stage starts to stagger around as if there were an earthquake. 'Rocks' (painted scrunched up newspaper or pieces of poly-styrene) are thrown at them from off stage.

Brandon: Whoa! What's happening?

Yasmin: I think the volcano is erupting!

Blessing: Quick! Back to the transporter!

Kyle: Hurry up! We need to get out of here.

Brandon, Yasmin and Blessing rush back to the transporter and Kyle pilots the craft off the volcano.

Blessing: Kyle? What are you doing here?

Kyle: Yasmin trapped me in the transporter when I helped her load the luggage.

Yasmin: Did I? Sorry, Kyle.

Kyle: Good job you did, otherwise you'd have been swallowed up by all that lava. Look at the volcano! Why didn't you check the data before you landed?

Blessing: Oh, er, I just thought we'd be better taking our own readings on the volcano.

Brandon: Thanks, Blessing. You almost got us all killed. Where's my sandwich suitcase, Yasmin? I need a banana and broccoli roll to recover.

Kyle: No time. We're about to land!

He mimes landing the craft and all get out. Blessing, Brandon and Yasmin stagger off stage.

Kyle: Oh, I'll just tidy all this up myself, shall I? Thanks, guys.

He picks up some bags and exits.

Experiment 2
The wonders of the universe

Yasmin emerges from the transporter, wearing a toolbelt and hard hat. She wipes her hands on a cloth.

Yasmin: (*Shouting off stage.*) Prof! Prof! It's all done now!

Rosalind: (*Entering.*) Excellent! Great work, Yasmin. With those modifications, the transporter can go anywhere in the solar system. Just think of where we can go!

Blessing and Brandon enter. Brandon is eating a sandwich.

Blessing: Brandon, what is on that sandwich? It looks revolting.

Brandon: It's one of my finest creations! It's got cheese and peas, cake and steak, sardines and beans and... coco pops.

Blessing: Eurgh, just keep it away from me.

Rosalind: Ah, Blessing. Brandon. You're just in time. Yasmin has finished the modifications to the transporter, meaning that we can send the Discovery team into space!

Brandon: Amazing! I've just perfected the freeze-dried sandwich! It's ideal for eating brie and buttercream sandwiches on the Moon.

Blessing: (*Staring at Brandon in disbelief, then turning back to Rosalind.*) That's amazing, Prof. Where are we off to first?

Rosalind: Yasmin, have you got the map?

Yasmin: Yes, Prof, I stored it in the transporter.

She goes to the transporter and rummages through a box. She throws various soft items (food packets, clothes, a teddy bear) over her shoulder before pulling out a chart. She takes it over to the others.

Rosalind: (*Unrolling the chart and holding it for the others to see.*) Right. Saturn is our destination. We need to get close enough to investigate its atmosphere.

Unseen by the others, Kyle comes on with a bucket full of cleaning equipment and notices the mess that Yasmin has left on the floor by the transporter.

Kyle: Who's done this? I've only just swept this floor and now there's all this mess!

He picks some of the things up, then gets into the transporter to put them away. He does this several times while the others are talking.

Blessing: (*Pointing at the chart.*) So our flight path takes us past Mars, through the Asteroid Belt, then we slingshot around Jupiter and finally make it to Saturn. Simple!

Brandon: Yasmin, did you pack everything into the transporter? Including that space bread I've been developing?

Yasmin: Yes, but it's starting to smell. What did you make it with?

Brandon: Spinach. And prawns. And Battenberg cake.

Blessing: (*Looking horrified.*) In what way is that space bread?

Brandon: It's green! Aren't all aliens green?

Blessing: I have no idea how you became a scientist.

At this point, Kyle picks up the final item and gets into the transporter to put it away. He goes around the back of the transporter, so that the others don't see him when they get in.

Rosalind: Time to go, team! I'll keep in radio contact, so let me know how the journey goes.

Blessing: Will do, Prof. Come on, everyone, let's go!

The team get into the transporter, not noticing that Kyle is still in there. Blessing and Brandon mime flicking switches and checking dials.

Blessing: Close cabin doors.

Yasmin: Closing cabin doors. (*She mimes doing this.*)

Blessing: Initiate retro thrusters.

Yasmin: Initiating retro thruster. (*She mimes doing this.*)

Brandon: Make Brandon a sandwich.

Yasmin: Making Brandon a sandwi— hang on, I'm not doing that!

Brandon: Worth a try. I've got my emergency sandwich here. (*He pulls a small roll from his pocket and bites into it.*) Mm. Strawberry and swordfish.

Yasmin tries not to be sick.

Blessing: Firing rockets and... lift off!

Kyle: (*Appearing from the back of the transporter.*) What's that noise? Have they started the roadworks outside the lab again?

Blessing: Kyle! What are you doing in here? We're on our way to Saturn!

Kyle: Saturn? I can't go to Saturn, I've got a dentist's appointment at 2.30! Turn around and take me back!

Blessing: We can't turn around. Our course is programmed in and I can't change it!

Brandon: What are you doing in here anyway?

Kyle: Well, someone had left a load of mess outside the transporter, so I was just putting everything back.

Yasmin: Oh, sorry, Kyle. That was me.

Brandon: Better sit down and enjoy the ride, Kyle. (*He points out of the window.*) Look – there goes Mars!

Yasmin: Look out, we're entering the Asteroid Belt!

Blessing: Hang on, I'll have to take evasive action.

Blessing steers hard right, then hard left. The others lean to the appropriate sides and shout things like 'Whoa!' and 'Hang on!'

Brandon: Here comes Jupiter! Round we gooooooo!

The crew all topple to one side, then back again.

Kyle: Look! There it is: the rings look amazing!

Brandon: I've always wanted to see Saturn!

Yasmin: (*Consulting her tablet.*) The Prof has just sent through some more data about our trip. She said that we need to beware of Saturn's moons. There's one, called Enceladus...

Brandon: Enchiladas? You mean I might get to taste a space-Mexican sandwich? I love enchiladas! Refried beans and jelly beans – that's my favourite filling!

Yasmin: (*Enunciating clearly.*) No! Enceladus. We're going to pass quite close to it. It has enormous geysers that shoot ice and other materials almost 500 km into space!

Blessing: Wow! That's amazing!

Kyle: (*Looking nervous.*) How close are we going to get to it?

Blessing: (*Checking her instruments.*) Oh, not too close. We're fine if nothing goes wrong!

Brandon: Time for another sandwich.

He takes another roll from his pocket but fumbles it. He tries to get hold of it but topples into Blessing.

Blessing: Brandon! What are you doing?

Everyone falls to one side and shouts out.

Blessing: You've knocked us off course! We're heading towards Enceladus!

Yasmin: (*Straining to look out of the window.*) And a geyser has started to erupt. It's coming straight for us.

The crew do their best Star Trek *acting as they tip from side to side.*

Blessing: We're in freefall!

Yasmin: We're spinning out of control.

Brandon: Blessing! Do something!

Blessing grabs the joystick and struggles to right the transporter. Eventually, they recover.

Yasmin: That was close.

Brandon: I need a lie down.

Kyle: (*Staring out of the window in wonder.*) Look! Look at all the stars! They're beautiful!

Yasmin: Yes, look, you can see the Milky Way!

Blessing: And there are some of the moons of Saturn. There's Titan!

Kyle: Oh, this is so much better than going to the dentist.

The radio crackles; we hear Rosalind's voice.

Rosalind: Blessing, are you receiving me? How's the voyage?

Blessing: (*Into a microphone or similar.*) Hey, Prof. We got knocked off course by an unexpected flying object. (*She glares at Brandon, who looks embarrassed.*) But we can see so much of the solar system, and beyond. And it's wonderful.

Rosalind: Well, take all the readings you can and come back. Now, I need to find Kyle. There's been a chemical spillage in the biolab. **Wonder Zone** out!

Kyle: Blessing, you've got to get me back. If I'm not there to clear that spillage, there won't be a biolab left!

Blessing: Hang on then, here we go!

The team do some more Star Trek*-style diving around and then climb out of the transporter chatting excitedly.*

Experiment 3
The colours of the rainbow

Rosalind walks on, speaking into a smartphone.

Rosalind: Yes, Prime Minister. Yes, I understand. Strange lights in the sky over the Houses of Parliament... Are you feeling OK, Prime Minister? Listen, go and have a lie down and I'll send the Discovery team over.

Kyle: (*Entering with a broom.*) Wotcha, Prof. How are things? Are you OK if I do a bit of sweeping?

Rosalind: Of course. Carry on.

Kyle starts sweeping. Yasmin, Blessing and Brandon enter. Brandon is eating a sandwich.

Yasmin: I don't know how your guts can cope with all those disgusting sandwiches. If I ate everything you ate, I think my intestines would leap up through my throat to try and escape.

Brandon: (*Slapping his stomach.*) Constitution of an ox, me!

Blessing: What? You've got four stomachs?

Brandon: Eh?

Yasmin: Oxen have four stomachs. They're called ruminants. I suppose it's one explanation of why you're able to eat those disgusting butties. What is it today?

Brandon: Crème brûlée, curds and whey, chicken pâté and lemon sorbet.

Yasmin tries not to be sick.

Rosalind: Right, Discovery team, we've had a call from the Prime Minister. She's reported that there are some strange green lights over the Houses of Parliament. (*She shows the smartphone to Blessing.*) And they're all over social media. You need to get over there straight away.

Blessing: Of course! Yasmin, bring the car around to the front. We'll go straight away.

Rosalind: No, you can't go by car, I'm afraid. If the **Wonder Zone** team turns up on the steps of Parliament, it will be all over the news and people will start to panic. You'll have to go underground.

Brandon: We'll all become spies! I'm sure I can sneak into Parliament without being seen. (*He starts to sneak around the stage, pretending to be a spy avoiding being seen. He falls over Kyle's broom and drops his sandwich.*)

Kyle: Look out! Oh no, you've got lemon sorbet all over the floor. I'll have to mop that up now.

Kyle leans the broom against the transporter and goes off to get a mop and bucket. Brandon gathers himself and his sandwich and gets to his feet. In doing so, he accidentally knocks the broom into the transporter.

Rosalind: No, we don't have to go in like spies. There's a series of tunnels linking **Wonder Zone** HQ to the Houses of Parliament. You'll have to go in the transporter. The tunnels are not often used, so travel carefully. It's very dark down there.

Kyle comes back in with a mop and bucket. He starts cleaning where Brandon dropped his sandwich.

Blessing: Right you are, Prof. Yasmin, go and get the torches and night-vision goggles. We've got to be ready for every eventuality.

Yasmin nods and exits.

Blessing: Right, Brandon, get the transporter ready. You'll need to switch it to subterranean mode.

Kyle: (*Noticing his broom is now in the transporter.*) Oh, how did that get there? (*He leans into the transporter to retrieve his broom.*)

Brandon: (*Walking backwards towards the transporter.*) No problem, Blessing.

Brandon, still walking backwards, collides with Kyle and pushes him into the transporter. He shrieks as he falls in.

Blessing: What was that noise? No, don't tell me, it was your stomach, wasn't it, Brandon?

Brandon: Well, chicken pâté does take some digesting. (*He carries on eating his sandwich.*)

Yasmin: (*Entering, carrying a box.*) I think I've got everything!

Blessing: Brilliant, let's go.

They all get in the transporter. They haven't noticed that Kyle is in there with them. Blessing starts up the transporter.

Blessing: Here we go!

Brandon: Dive, dive, dive!

Rosalind: (*Waving.*) Remember, mum's the word! (*She notices the mop.*) Oh, Kyle's left his mop behind. And there's still sorbet on the floor. (*She picks the mop and bucket up and starts to walk off stage.*) Kyle! Kyle! Where are you? (*She exits.*)

The team jostle along as the transporter 'dives' underground. If you can dim the lights at this point, do so. Otherwise, the team should pretend that it's dark and they can't see.

Blessing: Yasmin, get the torches out. It's getting dark.

Yasmin passes torches to the others and they switch them on. They go out almost immediately.

Brandon: Why won't they work?

Blessing: Did you check the batteries, Yasmin?

Yasmin: Well, no. You never said to check them.

Brandon: What scientist doesn't check their equipment before using it? What an idiot!

Blessing: Never mind, I'll use the auxiliary lights on the transporter. (*She mimes flicking the switch. Nothing happens.*) Well, these aren't working either. (*She mimes putting the brake on the transporter.*) Brandon, did you switch the transporter to subterranean mode?

Brandon: Er...

Yasmin: Oh, I see. Who's the idiot now? We can't see a thing!

Kyle, still unseen, groans. The others scream in surprise and look around.

Brandon: What was that?

Yasmin: I don't know.

Brandon: (*Panicking.*) It's giant mutant moles! We're going to become mole food!

Kyle: (*Sitting up, rubbing his head.*) Oh, my head.

The others: Kyle!

Yasmin: What you doing here?

Kyle: Well, the last thing I remember was trying to get my broom out of the transporter... and then I woke up here. Where are we and why is it so dark?

Blessing: We're on our way to the Houses of Parliament, but these two clowns forgot to check the equipment before we left. And now we don't have any lights or have any idea of where we're going.

Kyle: Wait, what are those lights up there?

As Kyle points out of the window, the ceiling of your space lights up with blue light. Use any stage or disco lights you have.

Kyle: Open the door. Let's take a look!

They get out and stare at the glowing ceiling.

Blessing: You know what this is: it's bioluminescence!

Brandon: Biolumi-what?

Blessing: Bioluminescence – the light from millions of arachnocampa luminosa – glow worms. They're usually native to New Zealand. I wonder how they got here.

Yasmin: Well, however they got here, they're going to light the way to Parliament. (*She points off stage.*) And do you know what? I think I can see the light at the end of the tunnel!

Blessing: Brilliant! Let's go. I wonder what lights the Prime Minister can see.

Brandon: Maybe it's arachnoc– arachnocam– glow worms!

Yasmin: Let's find out!

They all rush off.

Experiment 4
The creatures of the world

Rosalind walks on, speaking into a smartphone.

Rosalind: Yes, Prime Minister, it is unusual for the Northern Lights to be visible this far south. It's unusual, but not impossible... Of course, Ma'am, I'll let you know if there's anything else you need to know.

Kyle comes on with some spray, glaring at the floor as he goes.

Kyle: Where are they? I'll get the little vandals!

Rosalind: What are you doing?

Kyle: Ants have been at the sugar in the tea cupboard. And they've infested the biscuit tin! I'm going to spray them out of existence! (*He goes to spray something he's seen on the floor.*)

Rosalind: (*Going to stop him.*) Wait! You can't just wipe them out! It's not their fault. Did you close the sugar packet properly? Or the biscuit tin?

Kyle: Well I did, but I think Brandon left it open when he was making his sugar, shortbread and shepherd's pie sandwich.

Brandon and Blessing enter. Brandon is eating a sandwich.

Rosalind: And here is Brandon. Is that the offending sugar, shortbread and shepherd's pie sandwich?

Brandon: No, I finished that one ages ago. This one's crab sticks and pic 'n' mix! What do you mean 'offending'? My sandwiches aren't offensive!

Blessing: They're the most offensive things I've ever laid eyes on.

Kyle: What the Prof means, Brandon, is that when making your revolting meaty biscuit butty, you left the sugar open and the biscuit tin exposed to the ants! (*He walks over to Brandon and brandishes the spray in his face.*) And now we're overrun with the insects!

Brandon: Oh! Sorry. (*He pushes the spray bottle aside.*)

Yasmin: (*Coming on, wiping her hands on a cloth.*) I've finished all those miniaturisation settings on the transporter, Prof. Hopefully when we re-size back to normal, we won't be ten metres tall!

Rosalind: How is tiny Tim? Have we managed to return him to his normal size?

Yasmin: Not yet – he's still over three metres tall, but he's had several offers from basketball teams, so he's asked that we leave him as he is.

Rosalind: Splendid! Well, our insect problem seems the perfect chance to try it out! Team, I'd like you to shrink down and investigate where all the ants are coming from!

Blessing: Great!

Brandon: Er, wait a minute... what happens if we get stood on, or Kyle sprays us?

Rosalind: You'll be fine. We'll keep an eye on you and make sure no one goes near the area you're studying. And that includes Kyle and his bug spray.

Kyle: Humph!

Blessing: OK, team, everyone in the transporter.

Blessing, Brandon and Yasmin climb into the transporter and start their checks. Meanwhile, Kyle stares at the floor around him in increasing panic.

Kyle: Hey, Prof, I think these ants are ganging up on me! (*He backs up towards the transporter as if surrounded by ants.*) I think they know I'm the one with the spray!

Blessing: Miniaturising in three...

Kyle: (*Backing ever closer to the transporter in panic.*) Help me, Prof!

Blessing: Two...

Rosalind: Kyle, come away from the transporter!

Blessing: One...

Kyle: Prof! Help! Argh! (*He topples backwards into the transporter.*)

Blessing: Miniaturise!

Rosalind: Kyle!

Lights flash. The team all shout. Rosalind leaves the stage in the swirling light.

Yasmin: Kyle, what are you doing in here?

Brandon: Kyle, you made me drop my crab sticks!

Kyle: Let me out! Let me out!

Blessing: Too late, Kyle. We've miniaturised! We're the size of ants now.

Kyle: What? They were after me when I was normal size. Think what they'll do now I'm the same height as them!

Brandon: Calm down, Kyle. Have a bite of my sandwich. That'll make you feel better.

Kyle takes a bite and spits it out immediately.

Kyle: That's disgusting!

Blessing: Listen, Kyle. I'm sure they won't realise who you are. Leave that spray in here and let's go out and take a look.

They get out tentatively and creep across the stage. They look around and take readings on their smartphones.

Kyle: (*Looking off stage.*) I think there are some ants coming!

Some ants (actors dressed in black wearing ant masks) enter and run towards the group.

Kyle: They're coming to get me! (*He runs off in the opposite direction.*)

Yasmin: Kyle, wait!

They all run off, followed by the ants. A second later, Kyle runs across the stage and off the opposite side, followed by Yasmin, Blessing and Brandon, still eating his sandwich. They are pursued by the ants. A second later, the four of them run back the other way, followed by the ants. A second later, the ants run across followed by the team. On each pass, the team scream as they run. Finally the team come back on and stand together, panting and putting their hands on their knees.

Yasmin: (*Out of breath.*) I think we lost them.

Kyle: Phew! I thought they were going to get me and carry me off!

Brandon: Hang on, here they come again.

The 'ants' come on again, this time carrying large pieces of polystyrene. Kyle starts to run off, but Blessing grabs his arm.

Blessing: Wait! They're not chasing us! They're carrying sugar back to their nest!

Yasmin: (*Holding up a smartphone to take a reading.*) They're using smells to communicate with each other. They've laid a trail to the sugar bowl so that others can find it and take it away.

Kyle: They're going to steal all my sugar! (*To Brandon.*) And it's all your fault! I should have sprayed them all when I had the chance!

Blessing: Hey! No! If you sprayed them, then you would have killed half their nest. Ants are great for the environment. They speed up decomposition, they turn the soil and they disperse seeds!

Yasmin: All we need to do when we get back to normal size is move the sugar outside and make sure we keep the new sugar packet and biscuit tin properly closed.

Kyle: OK, but, Brandon, that means you have to keep everything closed.

Brandon: Well, I don't think sugar, shortbread and shepherd's pie is a winning combination. I'm going to try custard cream and cottage cheese next!

Blessing: Come on, let's get back to our normal size.

They all climb back into the transporter. Blessing flicks switches and they jostle and jiggle about in their seats, shouting as if they were on a rollercoaster. Finally, they sit back in their chairs, exhausted, then get out of the transporter.

Yasmin: Phew.

Brandon: Back to normal again. Oh no!

Blessing: What?

Brandon: (*Holding up a tiny breadstick.*) My sandwich is still miniature!

Kyle: Never mind, come on. I'll make you another. How about plain old ham?

Brandon: Just ham? Sounds revolting.

They exit.

Experiment 5
The possibilities of robots

For this episode, the transporter should have some kind of 'robotic' arm fitted to it. This could be a person disguised as part of the transporter, with their arm forming the robotic arm.

Rosalind enters speaking into a smartphone.

Rosalind: Prime Minister, calm down. Not everyone you see is a robot. Listen, I'll send the Discovery team to the Centre of Clever Robotics to investigate. (*She repeats the PM's question in surprise.*) How do you know I'm not a robot? Well, I suppose you don't, really. Listen, we'll clear it up, PM! Bye. Goodbye. (*She hangs up.*)

Yasmin: (*Entering, wiping her hands on a cloth.*) I've fitted those robotic attachments to the transporter. They should all be working fine now.

Rosalind: Excellent, Yasmin. I've just had a call from the Prime Minister. She is convinced everyone around her is a robot. I've told her I'd send the team to the Centre of Clever Robotics just to reassure her.

Blessing and Brandon enter. Brandon is eating a sandwich.

Brandon: (*To Blessing as they enter.*) I know those automated lunch machines are state of the art, but they'll never make the perfect sandwich, not with their programming. Sandwich making is an art; it's a gift. You need skill and talent, inspiration and creativity. You don't get that with artificial intelligence. (*He takes a large bite out of his sandwich.*)

Blessing: You know, sometimes I wonder if your intelligence is artificial.

Brandon: (*Holding up sandwich.*) But take this beauty. Frog's legs and fried eggs. No lunch machine could come up with that on its own.

Yasmin: That's because the lunch machines are programmed only to make edible sandwiches.

A voice is heard, as if over a public address system.

Voice: Kyle to the canteen. Kyle to the canteen. A lunch machine has exploded and sprayed egg mayonnaise all over the Minister for Science.

Everyone laughs at the announcement.

Rosalind: Right, team, we need to go to the Centre of Clever Robotics. The Prime Minister thinks everyone who works for her is a robot and we need to reassure her!

They gather around the transporter, as if to get everything ready. Rosalind exits.

Kyle: (*Rushing on with his cleaning bucket.*) Out of my way, everyone! Egg mayonnaise emergency! Cleaner coming through!

The team quickly get into the transporter to get out of his way. The robotic arm on the transporter springs to life and grabs Kyle. It drags him into the transporter.

Kyle: Argh! Let go of me! I need to clean the canteen!

Blessing: (*Miming flicking switches.*) Hang on! I'll get it to let go of you. (*Brandon wrestles with the arm to try and release it.*) It's not working. Yasmin! What did you do? Why won't the arm let him go?

Yasmin: I just fitted it according to the Centre of Clever Robotics' instructions. It's not meant to do this. (*She probes the arm with a screwdriver.*)

The team suddenly jostle and shudder as the transporter starts up.

Blessing: The transporter just started up of its own accord. What's happening?

Yasmin: What? It shouldn't do! I don't understand.

Robotic voice: Programming malfunction. Programming malfunction. Implementing repair protocol. Returning technology to the Centre of Clever Robotics for assessment.

The team do some Star Trek *acting, tipping from side to side as the transporter 'travels', shouting 'Help!', 'Whoa!' and similar as they do so. Then they suddenly stop. The arm lets go of Kyle.*

Brandon: Phew! Where are we?

Yasmin: (*Checking a smartphone.*) The Centre of Clever Robotics.

Blessing: Well, that's where we were going anyway, so I suppose it's worked out well.

Kyle: Not for me! I was going to the canteen to clean up a load of sandwich filling!

Brandon: My sandwich! (*He picks up a rather mangled looking package.*) Ruined!

An assistant dressed in a lab coat approaches the transporter.

Assistant: Welcome to the Centre of Clever Robotics. I have been sent by the director to bring you to his office.

Blessing: Oh right. Thanks.

Brandon: (*To assistant.*) Any idea how I can fix this sandwich?

Assistant: Apologies. I am programmed to research and test robotics. I have no programming for catering.

Kyle: Programming? You're a robot?

Yasmin: Fascinating. (*She takes out a magnifying glass and examines the assistant's face.*) The skin looks real!

Assistant: (*Ignoring Yasmin.*) This way, please.

The assistant leads the group around the stage. Other extras in lab coats walk across the stage. They nod to the assistant, who nods back.

Brandon: (*Amazed.*) Are all these people robots?

Assistant: Yes, there are many AI humanoids working at the Centre of Clever Robotics.

Kyle: AI?

Yasmin: Artificial intelligence.

A person in smart clothes enters. The assistant stops in front of them.

Assistant: Director, this is the team from the **Wonder Zone**.

Yasmin runs up to the director and examines their skin with her magnifying glass.

Yasmin: This is amazing. This humanoid's skin is even more realistic! They've even got spots!

Director: (*Pushing Yasmin away.*) Hey! I'm an actual human!

Blessing: (*Pushing past Yasmin to shake the director's hand.*) Director, lovely to meet you. We've had some issues with the new robotic elements of our transporter. Can your people, er robots, whatever... can they take a look at it?

Director: Of course, right away. (*They nod to the assistant, who exits.*)

Blessing: That's not why we came to see you. The Prime Minister is complaining about the number of AI humanoids at 10 Downing Street. She says they're acting strangely and she's worried about their programming. How many humanoids do you have stationed in Downing Street?

Director: (*Consulting a smartphone.*) Er, none. We have only installed automatic lunch machines.

Brandon: Really? Then what's the Prime Minister complaining about?

Director: Well, whatever strange behaviour the staff are exhibiting is purely their own choice. Our humanoids follow their programming. They are able to learn from their experience and develop their practices, but they won't behave weirdly.

Blessing: I wonder what's going on at Number 10, then?

Brandon: Whatever it is, they're all benefiting from my amazing sandwiches. I popped over yesterday and reprogrammed the lunch machines so that they can make my recipes. They can choose from bran flake and potato cake, sardine and tangerine or chocolate mousse and roasted goose.

Kyle: No wonder they're all acting strangely. They're probably all reacting to your terrible sandwiches!

Yasmin: We'd better get over there and reset the lunch machines.

Brandon: What? Some people have got no taste.

Director: I don't think your transporter is ready yet.

Kyle: Don't worry, we'll walk. I've had enough of that machine to last me a lifetime.

They all exit, with Brandon telling Blessing and Kyle about his sandwiches and Yasmin grilling the director about AI.

LAB EQUIPMENT 6

Other resources

Psalm 8

¹ Our Lord and Ruler,
your name is wonderful
  everywhere on earth!
You let your glory be seen
  in the heavens above.
² With praises from children
and from tiny infants,
  you have built a fortress.
It makes your enemies silent,
and all who turn against you
  are left speechless.

³ I often think of the heavens
  your hands have made,
and of the moon and stars
  you put in place.
⁴ Then I ask, "Why do you care
  about us humans?
Why are you concerned
  for us weaklings?"

⁵ You made us a little lower
  than you yourself,
and you have crowned us
  with glory and honour.
⁶ You let us rule everything
  your hands have made.
And you put all of it
  under our power—
⁷ the sheep and the cattle,
  and every wild animal,
⁸ the birds in the sky,
the fish in the sea,
  and all ocean creatures.

⁹ Our Lord and Ruler,
your name is wonderful
  everywhere on earth!

Contemporary English Version © 1997 Bible Society

Psalm 104

¹ I praise you, Lord God,
   with all my heart.
You are glorious and majestic,
dressed in royal robes
   ² and surrounded by light.
You spread out the sky
   like a tent,
³ and you built your home
   over the mighty ocean.
The clouds are your chariot
   with the wind as its wings.
⁴ The winds are your
      messengers,
and flames of fire
   are your servants.

⁵ You built foundations
for the earth, and it
   will never be shaken.
⁶ You covered the earth
with the ocean that rose
   above the mountains.
⁷ Then your voice thundered!
And the water flowed
   ⁸ down the mountains
and through the valleys
   to the place you prepared.
⁹ Now you have set
      boundaries,
so that the water will never
   flood the earth again.

¹⁰ You provide streams of
      water
   in the hills and valleys,
¹¹ so that the donkeys
and other wild animals
   can satisfy their thirst.
¹² Birds build their nests
      nearby
   and sing in the trees.
¹³ From your home above
you send rain on the hills
   and water the earth.
¹⁴ You let the earth produce
grass for cattle,
plants for our food,
¹⁵ wine to cheer us up,
olive oil for our skin,
and grain for our health.

¹⁶ Our Lord, your trees
   always have water,
and so do the cedars
   you planted in Lebanon.
¹⁷ Birds nest in those trees,
and storks make their home
   in the fir trees.
¹⁸ Wild goats find a home
   in the tall mountains,
and small animals can hide
   between the rocks.

¹⁹ You created the moon
   to tell us the seasons.
The sun knows when to set,
²⁰ and you made the
      darkness,
so the animals in the forest
   could come out at night.
²¹ Lions roar as they hunt
   for the food you provide.
²² But when morning comes,
   they return to their dens,
²³ then we go out to work
   until the end of day.

²⁴ Our Lord, by your wisdom
   you made so many things;
the whole earth is covered
   with your living
      creatures.
²⁵ But what about the ocean
   so big and wide?
It is alive with creatures,
   large and small.
²⁶ And there are the ships,
   as well as Leviathan,
the monster you created
   to splash in the sea.

Contemporary English Version © 1997 Bible Society

LAB EQUIPMENT

Animal and people shapes

Diffraction goggles

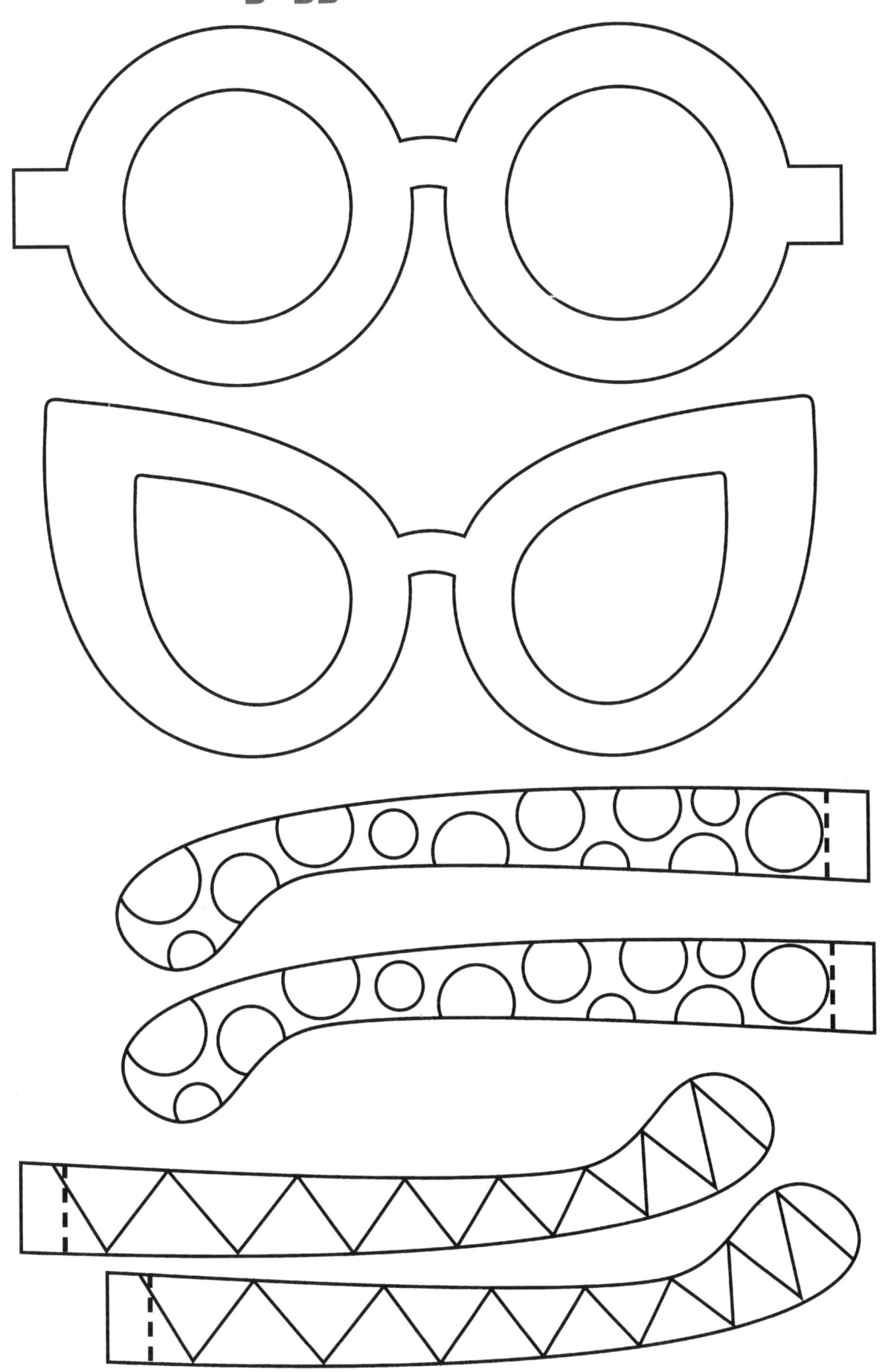

LAB EQUIPMENT

Moving figures

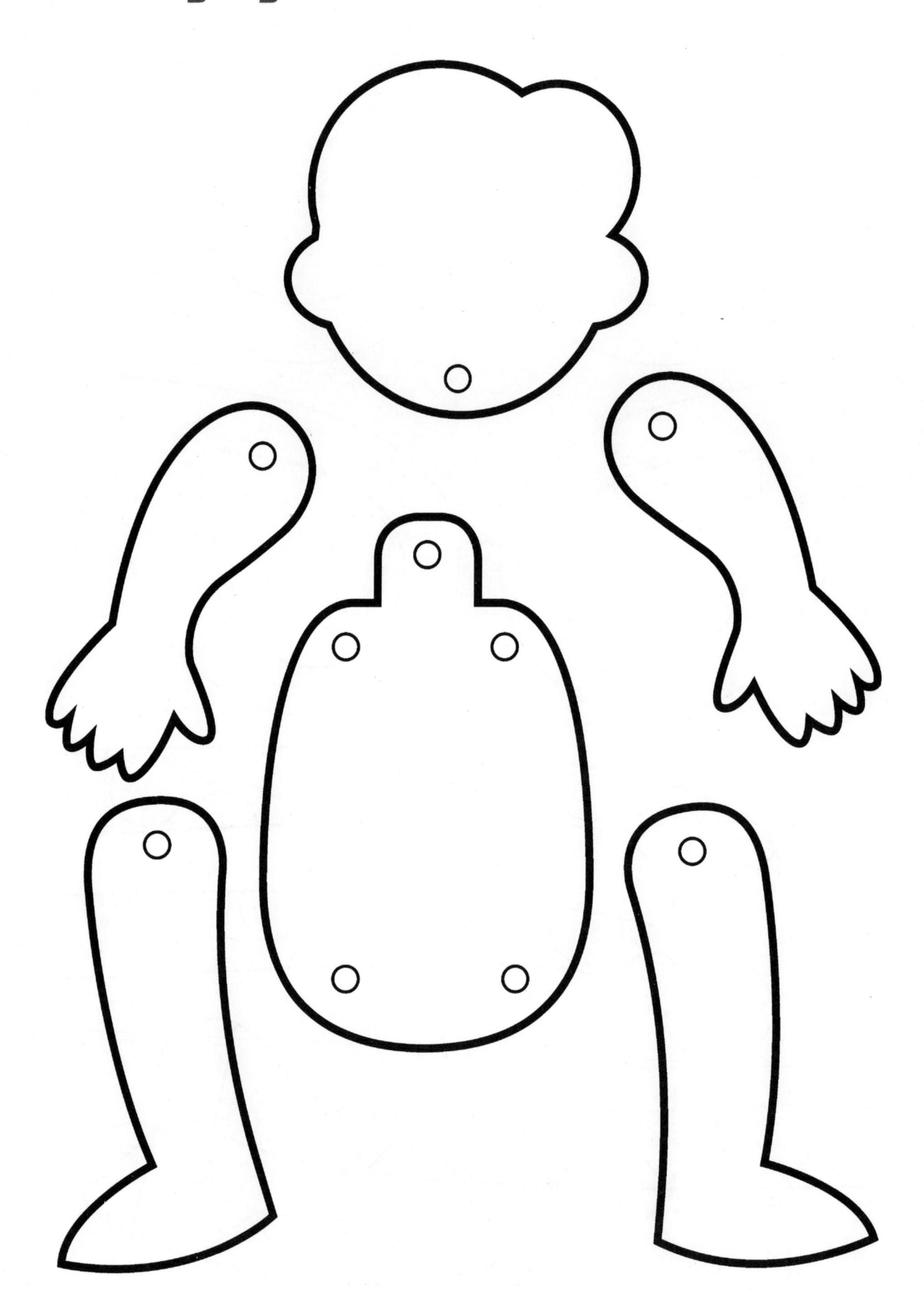

92

It's a Wonderful, Wonderful World
The Wonder Zone theme song

Doug Horley and Andrew Chevalier

Capo 3 (D)   Key = F

♩ = 80

Intro — | D A | Bm G | D A | Bm G | *Chorus*
(F C | Dm B♭ | F C | Dm B♭)

It's a

% D | A | Bm | G
   F | C | Dm | B♭

won-der-ful, won-der-ful, won-der-ful, won-der-ful, won - der-ful, won-der-ful world. It's an

D | A | Bm G | D A
F | C | Dm B♭ | F C

ut-ter-ly mar - vel-lous, to - tal-ly glo - ri-ous, sim - ply in-cre - di-ble world. And as

D | A | Bm | G
F | C | Dm | B♭

we stand a-mazed_ we will sing_ out in praise_ to the God___who made it all:_ this

Last time to Coda 2 ⊕ ⊕

D | A | Bm | G
F | C | Dm | B♭

mar - vel-lous, glo - ri - ous, glo - ri-ous, won - der-ful, won - der-ful world_____ oh,_ oh, oh._ This

93

mar-vel-lous, glo-ri-ous, won-der-ful, won-der-ful world.
1. He made it
2. He made it

all work to-ge-ther in ways that blow our minds, with
all work to-ge-ther in ways that blow our minds, with

whales and snails and fin-ger-nails and crea-tures of all kinds. His han-di-
trees and seas and gra-vi-ty and won-ders of all kinds. His han-di-

work's all a-round us and plain for all to see, from out-
work's all a-round us and plain for all to see; he's one

-er space to the nose sat on my face he made it all. It's a
who cares, so he e-ven counts the hairs up-on my head.

Copyright © 2019 Scripture Union
Administration by Song Solutions www.songsolutions.org
CCLI 7132547

It's a wonderful, wonderful world

It's a wonderful, wonderful, wonderful, wonderful, wonderful, wonderful world.
It's an utterly marvellous, totally glorious, simply incredible world.
And as we stand amazed, we will sing out in praise
To the God who made it all:
This marvellous, glorious, wonderful, wonderful world,
This marvellous, glorious, wonderful, wonderful world.

He made it all work together in ways that blow our minds,
With whales and snails and fingernails and creatures of all kinds.
His handiwork's all around us and plain for all to see,
From outer space to the nose sat on my face he made it all.

He made it all work together in ways that blow our minds,
With trees and seas and gravity and wonders of all kinds.
His handiwork's all around us and plain for all to see;
He's one who cares, so he even counts the hairs upon my head.

W O N D E R it's wonder, wonderful.
W O N D E R it's wonder, wonderful.
W O N D E R it's wonder, wonderful.
W O N D E R it's wonder, wonderful.

© Doug Horley 2019